A HISTORY OF THE CHILEAN BOUNDARIES

A HISTORY
OF
THE
CHILEAN
BOUNDARIES

★

ROBERT D. TALBOTT

A Replica Edition

THE IOWA STATE UNIVERSITY PRESS
Ames, Iowa
1974

ROBERT D. TALBOTT is associate professor of Latin American History, University of Northern Iowa, Cedar Falls.

© 1974 The Iowa State University Press
Ames, Iowa 50010. All rights reserved

Printed in the U.S.A.

First edition, 1974

International Standard Book Number: 0-8138-0305-5

Library of Congress Catalog Card Number: 74-3525

The Iowa State University Press REPLICA EDITIONS, reproduced directly from original typescript, are specialized studies selected for their significance and scholarly appeal.

CONTENTS

FOREWORD

THERE has never been a complete history of the Chilean boundaries,
and almost all the works that do exist on the subject are written from a
partisan point of view. Chilean authors have written extensively about the
sections involved in boundary disputes in order to justify the Chilean position. Accounts written by the historians of other countries involved in the
disputes are just as partisan and incomplete. Few people outside of Latin
America have treated the subject at all. Only the Tacna-Arica arbitration
and the Argentine-Chilean Boundary arbitration have received much attention by the historians of any country. Colonial boundaries have been discussed only in so far as they validate national claims, and no discussion of
the entire boundary exists for any period.

Colonial boundary changes, that portion of the Argentine-Chilean
boundary that was not disputed, and the Puna de Atacama region have been
neglected. The Puna de Atacama and the part of the Andes boundary determined by mutual agreement constitute about one-half of Chile's frontier,
but these areas have attracted little interest because they were not the subject of a violent disagreement. Nevertheless, they are a necessary part of
a complete boundary discussion.

The colonial boundaries are particularly important in South America
because they form the basis on which national boundaries are established.
When the Spanish colonies in South America proclaimed their independence,
they accepted as their frontiers those which they possessed as Spanish
colonies. This principle, called the uti posidetis of 1810, became the accepted rule for boundary demarcation in South America. Both Chile and
Argentina based their claims to Patagonia and the Strait of Magellan upon
colonial titles and the principle of the uti posidetis of 1810.

The Spanish sovereigns usually named natural features such as deserts or mountains as the boundaries between the divisions of their empire
in South America. For this reason, frontier areas rather than definite
boundary lines were established in the colonial period. When the independent states expanded into the border areas, boundary disputes arose.

vii

Chile, lying between the Pacific Ocean on the west and the Andes Mountains on the east, expanded to the north and to the south. Her northern expansion resulted from the discovery of nitrates in the Desert of Atacama during the 1830's. By the end of the nineteenth century, nitrates constituted an important factor in the economic life of Chile. They had become the largest source of government revenue.

When Chile expanded into the Desert of Atacama, a colonial frontier area, she became involved in a boundary controversy with Bolivia which resulted in the War of the Pacific, 1879-1883. As a result of defeating Bolivia and Peru, Chile obtained not only the Bolivian littoral but also control over the Peruvian provinces of Tacna and Arica. The Tacna-Arica question arising from the War of the Pacific involved Chile and Peru in a bitter dispute which lasted until 1929. Chile had obtained control but not sovereignty over the provinces. A plebiscite to be held ten years after the signing of the Treaty of Ancón in 1884 was supposed to determine which nation should have sovereignty over the area, but the two countries could not agree upon conditions for holding the plebiscite. The question of the plebiscite led to the rupture of diplomatic relations in 1910. Finally, the United States' offer of arbitration in 1922 was accepted. A direct settlement, resulting from the arbitration attempt, ended the problem in 1929. Peru received Tacna, and Chile retained Arica.

As she expanded southward, Chile encountered a boundary problem with Argentina. In 1842 Chile founded a colony in the Strait of Magellan. Argentina claimed the Strait area, and the two nations negotiated until 1881 when a boundary treaty was signed. Disagreement over the principle of demarcation stated in the Treaty of 1881 almost led to war. Then, in 1903, the boundary north of 52° S. latitude was determined by the arbitration of Queen Victoria and King Edward VII. In the post World War II years border incidents occurred in this area where the boundary had been previously settled because of disagreement over the locations of the boundary markers. Although relations between the two nations became strained, a peaceful settlement was arranged in 1965 by an agreement to establish a joint border commission to mark the boundary in the Laguna del Desierto region fifty miles north of the Strait and by an accord submitting the Palena Valley area near Chiloé to arbitration by Queen Elizabeth II. A dispute in the Puna de Atacama developed after World War II but subsided without an agreement.

One minor area remains in dispute at the present time, three islands in the Beagle Channel. No settlement has been reached to date, and tensions have become more serious as a result of the extension of naval activity by both nations into the Beagle Channel area since 1954.

viii

Boundary problems, which have continued throughout the period of Chile's independence, constitute a considerable portion of the history of Chile. They have been the main concern of Chilean diplomacy for the last one hundred years. In determining her boundaries Chile has resorted to war, arbitration, and direct agreement. Boundary problems have also played an important part in the economic life of the country.

I owe a special debt of gratitude to my wife, who assisted in research and in editing the manuscript. The time necessary for the completion of this manuscript was made possible by a research appointment granted by the University of Northern Iowa.

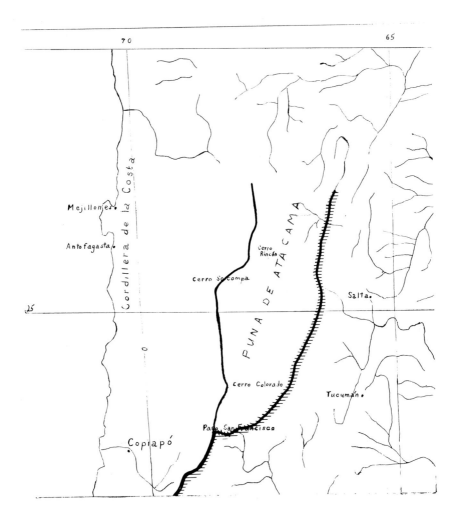

X

LA RIOJA

30 Coquimbo

SAN JUAN

San Juan

Paso Aconcagua   Mendoza

VALPARAISO   San Luis

SANTIAGO   SAN LUIS

Paso Las Damas   Rio Diamante

35   MENDOZA

GOBERNACION

Concepción

DE LA PAMPA

xi

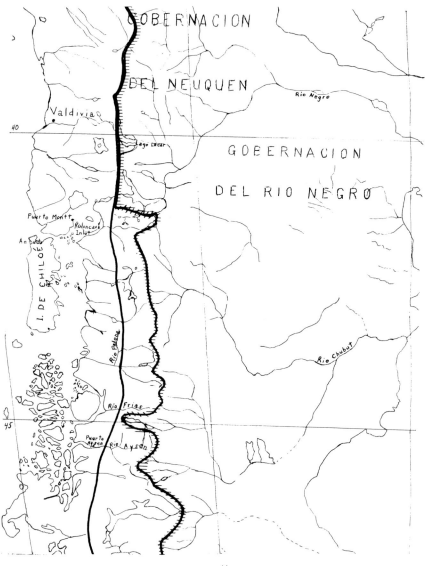

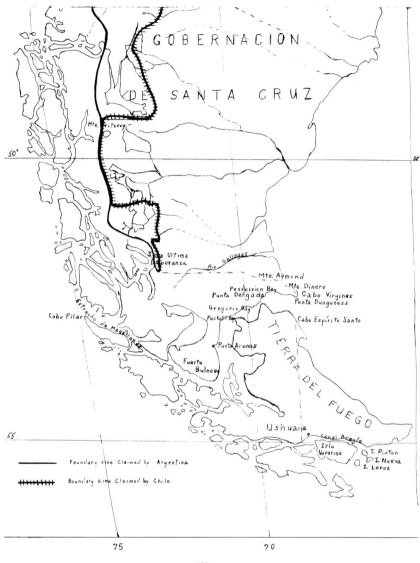

GOBERNACION

DE SANTA CRUZ

Mte. Fitzroy

50°

Seno Ultima
Esperanza

Rio Gallegos

Mte. Aymond

Possession Bay
Punta Delgada
Mte. Dinero
Cabo Virgines
Punta Dungeness

Gregorio Bay
Peckett Bay

Cabo Espírito Santo

Cabo Pilar

Estrecho de Magallanes

Punta Arenas

Fuerte
Bulnes

TIERRA DEL FUEGO

Ushuaia

Canal Beagle

Isla
Navarino

I. Picton
I. Nueva
I. Lenox

55

—————— Boundary Line Claimed by Argentina

+++++++++ Boundary Line Claimed by Chile

75

70

xiii

A HISTORY OF THE CHILEAN BOUNDARIES

CHAPTER 1. COLONIAL PERIOD

DURING the colonial period the boundaries of the Captaincy General of Chile gradually expanded into areas determined by geographic conditions. Sparsely populated or uninhabited territories separated Chile from her neighbors and eliminated any necessity for exact determination of boundary lines. The Cordillera of the Andes on the east, separating Chile from the Rio de la Plata provinces, and the Desert of Atacama on the north, separating Chile from Peru and Alto Peru, served as the border areas. In addition, the Spanish crown did not consider exact boundaries necessary to mark off the administrative subdivisions within the empire. Whatever boundaries for division within the empire were established by the crown were in cedulas granting territories to individuals. The first boundaries for Chile were included in a cedula dated at Toledo on July 26, 1529.[1] The cedula contained the terms of the capitulation between the crown and Simón de Alcazaba for the discovery, conquest, and colonization of lands between Peru and the Strait of Magellan.

Simón de Alcazaba was a Portuguese navigator who had served his native country in the East Indies for several years. Because he did not get the recognition and opportunity he wanted, Alcazaba transferred to the service of Spain. Charles I selected Alcazaba as a delegate to the Badajos Conference of March, 1524, which was called to settle the dispute over the Spice Islands that had been pending for thirty years, since the Treaty of Tordesilla of 1494. Charles I considered Alcazaba a valuable expert because of his first-hand knowledge of the area. However, John III of Portugal objected to the appointment, and Charles rescinded it.

After Alcazaba was dismissed as a delegate to the Badajos Conference, he was appointed commander of the second relief expedition which Charles intended to send to the Molucca Islands, part of the Spice Islands, to aid the Loaysa-del Cano expedition of 1525. Garcia Jofre Loaysa and Juan Sebastian del Cano, the man who had successfully brought the survivors of the Magellan voyage back to Spain, attempted unsuccessfully in the 1525 voyage to establish trade with the Spice Islands through the Strait of Magellan. The first relief expedition under the command of Sebastian Cabot got no farther than the Río de la Plata before returning to Spain. The second relief expedition, which was given to Alcazaba to command, was canceled when Charles sold his claims to the Spice Islands to the King of Portugal in April, 1529.

Alcazaba, who was an older man, began to feel that time was running out for him. An ambitious man, he had left the service of his own country with the firm expectation that the Spanish king would offer him greater opportunities. Because each of his assignments had been canceled, Alcazaba believed that Charles should give first consideration to his request for New World territory to conquer. Alcazaba's claim to Charles's consideration was helped by the presence of powerful friends at court, including the Bishop of Ciudad Rodrigo.

Charles accepted the petition of Alcazaba and in July of 1529 granted him an area from Chincha two hundred leagues south to the Strait of Magellan. Chincha, located on the Peruvian coast about 14° S., was the southern boundary of the territory granted by the crown to Francisco Pizarro. On the same day she signed the capitulation with Alcazaba, Queen Isabel, acting as regent during the absence of her husband, signed a cedula granting Peru to Pizarro.[2] The boundaries of Peru extended from Tenumpuela about 2° S. to Chincha. No eastern boundary was established for the Alcazaba grant.

Since the league used was based upon the measurement of seventeen and one half leagues per degree longitude at the equator, a league equals 3.4 miles.[3] Alcazaba's grant, therefore, was not quite seven hundred miles long. Alcazaba maintained that the distance between Chincha and the Strait was seven hundred leagues instead of two hundred. He petitioned the crown to permit him to choose two hundred leagues within the area.[4] Alcazaba also was having trouble trying to find financing for a colonizing expedition; the wealth of Peru was the center of attention in Spain at that time.

In May, 1534, King Charles decided to reorganize the grants he had previously awarded in South America, including the one given to Alcazaba. The Spanish portion of South America was divided into four parts. Pizarro's lands were extended about seventy leagues farther south from Chincha and east to the Demarcation Line between the Spanish and Portuguese Empires.[5] At the same time the king signed three additional cedulas granting lands to Diego de Almagro, Pedro de Mendoza, and Alcazaba.[6] The present territory of Chile was included in the western portion of these three grants.

Diego de Almagro, Pizarro, and Fernando Luque, schoolmaster and vicar-general of the church in Darien, had combined their resources for the conquest of Peru. As compensation for his contributions to the conquest of Peru, Almagro was granted the two hundred leagues of territory adjoining the Pizarro grant on the south. This was the area that had earlier been conceded to Alcazaba by the queen regent in 1529. The two hundred leagues of land south of Almagro's grant were given to Pedro de Mendoza, an influential noble in the Spanish court. This area included the Río de la Plata since the three southern grants extended from the Atlantic Ocean to the Pacific Ocean.

The fourth and southern-most grant was given to Alcazaba. Alcazaba's new grant was the two hundred leagues of territory located between Mendoza's lands and the Strait of Magellan. Under the terms of the grant Alcazaba was required to send to his territory an expedition of one hundred fifty men within six months and another expedition of one hundred men within a year and a half from the departure date of the first expedition.

Simón de Alcazaba prepared the first expedition and sailed from Sanlúcar de Barrameda on September 21, 1534. [7] Two ships, the Madre de Dios and the San Pedro, with one hundred sixty-nine men comprised this first colonizing effort. On January 18, 1535, the fleet entered the Strait of Magellan after a difficult voyage lasting almost four months. Alcazaba sailed about one-third of the way through the Strait to the Island of the Ducks, which is now called Elizabeth or Penguin Island. Here he stopped for a short time to kill a few hundred penguins to replenish the food supply. He remained in the Strait approximately two weeks exploring the area before sailing to Port of Lions situated on a bay near the Cape of San Domingo, 45° S., on the Atlantic coast. Alcazaba chose this site as the headquarters of his colony. He was immediately sworn in as governor.

Four days later, on February 9, Alcazaba led a party inland to explore and to seek wealth. Because of age and corpulence, Alcazaba found the hardships of overland travel too difficult and after two days returned to the ships. The remaining members of the inland expedition traveled for twenty-two days toward the northwest and north for about thirty-four leagues. They experienced much suffering from thirst and hunger but discovered only a few natives and no wealth.

Three days after the exploring party began the return trip, Captains Juan Arias and Gaspar de Sotelo mutinied and gained control of the party. The two rebellious captains sent an advance squad to seize Alcazaba and to take control of the ships. The small advance party did succeed in capturing the ships by surprise; Alcazaba was stabbed in his bed and thrown overboard.

A disagreement between the two rebel leaders enabled the master of the <u>Madre de Dios</u> to regain control and to hang the mutineers after a trial aboard ship. The expedition by this time was suffering from disappointment and low morale as well as loss of leadership and manpower. A total of eighty men were lost aboard ship, on the inland expedition, and by execution. Consequently, it was decided to wait until June 17 for stragglers to return from the interior and then return to Spain. On the return voyage the expedition landed in Brazil in July and in Santo Domingo in September before sailing for Spain.

The first colonizing attempt in the Strait of Magellan ended in failure: Alcazaba lost his life; no wealth was found; and the Strait area did not present an attraction of any kind. In fact, although the purpose of the effort was the exploration of the Strait area, most of the activity was not within the Strait.

In the latter part of the century a second attempt to colonize in the Strait itself was made by Pedro Sarmiento de Gamboa. Sarmiento was born about 1532 and grew up in Galicia near the west coast. He was familiar with the sea and grew to like it. When he reached eighteen, Sarmiento entered military service and served in both the Spanish army and navy. Between 1550 and 1555 Sarmiento saw duty in the army in Europe; then he entered the navy, serving in the Caribbean area for two years. Upon leaving the navy, Sarmiento remained in the New World and within a short time went to Peru where he entered the service of the Viceroy, the Marqués de Cañete. His knowledge and ability earned him the respect of secular officials and a position at the viceregal court, where he continued to serve succeeding viceroys. During the administration of Lope García de Castro, who was in office from 1564 to 1569, Sarmiento explored extensively in the Pacific as far west as the Soloman Islands.

In 1569 Francisco de Toledo became viceroy and completed the pacification of Peru by discrediting Inca traditions and by eliminating the Inca royal family in order to do away with any rival authority. As part of this campaign Viceroy Toledo commissioned Sarmiento to collect information from surviving Inca officials and learned men and to write an account of the Incas. The history of the Incas which Sarmiento wrote was biased against the Incas and extremely favorable to the Spanish conquerors. This prejudice, which was recognized in Spain, delayed publication for several years. Viceroy Toledo valued Sarmiento's services so much that he protected him from the Inquistion, which on two occasions ordered Sarmiento banished from Peru after twice finding him guilty of witchcraft and blasphemy.

By the time Francis Drake arrived at Callao on his raiding expedition in 1579, Sarmiento was held in high esteem by Viceroy Toledo. Be-

cause of the military and civil services he had already performed and because of his knowledge of the Pacific, Sarmiento was chosen to command
the expedition which unsuccessfully gave chase to Drake. Following the
failure to overtake Drake, Viceroy Toledo decided to send an expedition
to the Strait of Magellan to intercept Drake and to investigate the possibility of fortifying this passage to prevent other raiders from using it.
Sarmiento was appointed to command the expedition to the Strait.

The Strait expedition, consisting of two ships, the Nuestra Señora
de Esperanza and the San Francisco, with crews totaling one hundred eighty
persons and a few Indian servants, sailed from Callao on October 11, 1579.[8]
Five weeks later, after sighting the Gulf of Trinity, Sarmiento began
searching for the Pacific entrance to the Strait. As he sailed southward
Sarmiento explored and mapped the area. On January 23, 1580, the western entrance to the Strait was reached and the work continued into the
Strait. Sites for a fort on each side of the Strait were selected. Sarmiento
decided that colonization was practical and necessary to support the forts.
He sailed on February 24 to report to the king and to request permission
to colonize the Strait.

After hearing the favorable report of Sarmiento, Philip II decided
to fortify the Strait and accepted Sarmiento's offer to finance colonization
of the area. The king appointed Sarmiento Governor and Captain General
of the Strait and sent at crown expense soldiers and materials for the forts.
Sarmiento organized an expedition of twenty-three ships with three thousand persons and sailed from Sanlúcar de Barrameda on September 17,
1581. Two hundred soldiers for the forts and six hundred colonists bound
for Chile under the leadership of don Alonso de Sotomayor, the new governor of Chile, were included in the expedition.

Bad luck plagued the colonizing effort from the start. On the third
day out a storm forced the fleet into the port of Cádiz and resulted in the
loss of five ships and eight hundred people. After the storm damage was
repaired the voyage was resumed with two hundred twenty-four settlers
and ten friars bound for the colony in the Strait and don Alonso and the colonists bound for Chile. During the winter months the expedition remained
in Brazil where serious difficulties developed between Sarmiento and Diego Flores de Valdés, General of the Fleet. The two leaders of the expedition had never been able to work together amiably, and the situation was
exacerbated by the fact that Flores was not as dedicated to the project as
Sarmiento was. In Brazil Flores was responsible for the loss of supplies
for the colony; and while they were still in port, Sarmiento accused him
of dereliction of duty.

An open rupture between the leaders occurred on the voyage to the

7

Strait. The fleet sailed from Rio de Janeiro in the spring of 1582 with only
two hundred six colonists; death and desertions accounted for the reduction.
One part of the fleet led by Flores wanted to give up and return to Spain,
but Sarmiento's consent was needed. This he refused to give; he insisted
upon continuing to the Strait. Storms and dissension resulting in desertions
caused a loss of ten ships during the voyage to the Strait. When the mouth
of the Strait came into view, Flores turned about and sailed for Rio de Janeiro. Sarmiento was unable to stop him or prevent the remaining ships,
including his own, from following.

In Rio de Janeiro General Flores deserted and returned to Spain.
Sarmiento reassembled the remaining men and ships, purchased an additional ship, recruited reinforcements, and again set sail for the Strait
with six ships on December 2, 1583. Two months later, after a stormy
voyage and the loss of one vessel, Sarmiento took the fleet into the Strait.
On February 11, 1584, Nombre de Jesús was founded in the Valley of the
Fountains at the entrance to a ravine one-half league from the Cape of
Virgins. In the middle of February the Trinidad was wrecked in an attempt to beach it to unload the cargo. The ship was a total loss, and most
of the cargo was lost too. Three days after this accident three of the remaining four ships sailed away after nightfall without notice. Sarmiento
then sailed in the one remaining ship to the center of the Strait. Twenty-
four leagues into the Strait the second narrows is located. Here the Strait
in only one-half league wide. Sarmiento chose this area as the site of one
of the two forts to be constructed to fortify the passage. Nearby on Point
Santa Ana he founded the second town, Rey don Felipe, on March 25, 1584.
For one month Sarmiento prepared the new colony for the approaching winter before sailing back to Nombre de Jesús. He arrived after dark, too
late to land. During the night a severe storm broke and blew the ship out
of the Strait. Sarmiento was compelled to make for Brazil.

In Brazil Sarmiento made arrangements for sending a supply ship
to aid the Strait settlements and then sailed for Spain in August, 1584. He
hoped to obtain aid for the colonies from the king. In September Sarmiento
was shipwrecked at Bahía, Brazil, and forced to return to Rio de Janeiro.
Here he learned that the supply ship had been forced by bad weather, characteristic of the winters in this area, to return to Rio de Janeiro without
completing its mission to the Strait. Even if the season for sailing south
had not been past, Sarmiento would not have had the money or credit to finance another relief expedition; so he decided that it was necessary to go
to Spain to obtain help for the Strait colonies. He embarked for Spain in
April, 1586. During this voyage Sarmiento and his ship were captured by
Sir Walter Raleigh. To prevent his papers from falling into the hands of

the English, he threw overboard all of his records including the maps and notes on the Strait. Sir Walter Raleigh sent Sarmiento to England as a prisoner.

Through Sir Walter Raleigh, Sarmiento obtained an audience with Queen Elizabeth at Windsor Castle. During the course of the two and one-half hour interview, Sarmiento impressed the Queen with his intelligence and honorable behavior. Queen Elizabeth chose him as her personal messenger to Philip II, granted him his freedom, and provided him with funds for the journey to Spain. In October, 1586, Sarmiento left London and crossed the English Channel to France to travel overland to his homeland. In the South of France, between Bordeaux and Bayonne, Sarmiento encountered yet another delay. He was taken captive by a group of Huguenots under the leadership of Captain de Vendôme, Vicomte de Béarne. For three years he was detained at Monte Marsan until a ransom could be sent from Spain. Upon his release Sarmiento proceeded to the Spanish court and arrived six years after leaving Brazil. During the nine years between the departure of Sarmiento from Spain to colonize the Strait and his return, Philip II had lost interest in the Strait and refused to provide any further assistance. Sarmiento was unable to do any more, and the Strait colonies were forgotten. Death by starvation or at the hands of the Indians was the fate of all four hundred colonists except one. The single survivor, Tomé Hernández, was picked up by Thomas Cavendish as he passed through the Strait to raid along the Pacific coast as Sir Francis Drake had done earlier. The English renamed Rey Don Felipe, Port Famine in memory of the fate of the colonists, and that is the name that has been remembered. This experience gave the Strait a bad reputation, and no further attempts to colonize this area, which had been granted first to Alcazaba and then to Sarmiento, were made during the colonial period.

In the grant adjoining Alcazaba's on the north there was greater success in colonizing. Pedro de Mendoza organized in 1534 and 1535 an expedition to colonize the Río de la Plata area granted to him by Charles I. Included in this expedition was a ship belonging to Flemish merchants located in Seville. Along with their ship these merchants sent their agent, Ulrich Schmidt, also called Schmidel. Schmidt remained in the New World almost twenty years before returning to Germany. His account of his years in the Río de la Plata area is quite valuable although it contains errors;[9] he wrote it from memory twenty years after the events occurred. One example of the inexactness of Mr. Schmidt's memory is the date of departure. Schmidt wrote that the expedition sailed September 1, 1534, instead of one year later, 1535.[10]

The primary interest of Mendoza and his party in the Río de la

Plata area was the search for an easy access to Peru and the great wealth of the Inca Empire. Exploration and colonization centered in Paraguay and along the river. No attention was given to the western part of the grant located in Chile. The western area was separated by the Andes from the section explored by the Mendoza company. This separation and the fact that the West was neglected by Mendoza led to that part of the grant located in present-day Chile later being designated a new, separate grant.

In the same period that Mendoza began colonizing up the Río de la Plata, Diego de Almagro began exploring the western portion of the same grant. With the permission of Francisco Pizarro, Almagro left Peru with four hundred men and about 15,000 Indian servants and bearers to explore Chile in search for wealth that hopefully would equal the riches of Peru. On the journey over the Andes and through the Desert of Atacama to Copiapó, more than eight hundred men, almost all of them Indians, died. After a short pause at Copiapó to recover, the party continued to the Valley of Aconcagua where they met Pedro Calvo, a fugitive from justice, who had fled Peru a few years before. Calvo had been accepted by the Indians and was living among them. He persuaded the Indians to welcome his countrymen and to adopt Christianity. Therefore, Almagro experienced no difficulties with the Indians in northern Chile.

Trouble with the Indians did develop farther south. Almagro sent a party of two hundred under Gomez de Alvarado exploring southward. The advance party proceeded to the Itata River where it encountered hostile activities by the Indians. As punishment and a warning Gomez de Alvarado and his men killed a large number of Indians, giving rise to a long-lasting hatred for the Spaniards that caused a great deal of trouble for those who later came to Chile. No wealth was discovered, and the advance party rejoined the main group at the site of present-day Santiago. The failure to find wealth and the hostility of the southern Indians made Almagro decide to return to Peru where wealth had already been discovered. Almagro elected to return to Peru by the coastal route through the Desert of Atacama as the lesser of two evils rather than brave the difficulties of the Andes again.

After his return to Peru in early 1537, Almagro became involved in a bitter dispute with Pizarro over the division of the Peruvian spoils. Almagro felt that he was being cheated out of his just reward by Francisco Pizarro and his brothers. Pizarro had been joined by his two brothers, Hernando and Gonzalo; and Almagro, probably with a great deal of justification, thought that the Pizarros were attempting to keep for themselves and their followers nearly all of the wealth of the Inca Empire. In the civil war that resulted, Almagro was captured and jailed. On July 8, 1538, by

10

order of Hernando Pizarro, Almagro was garroted in his jail cell and his body was decapitated in the public square.

With the death of Almagro his grant became vacant, and the Chilean territory could again be given to another conquistador for exploration and colonization. However, Chile was generally considered an undesirable area. Almagro's expedition had found no wealth and had encountered Indian troubles. Chile was said to be cold, uninhabitable except for savages, poor, and unable to support conquering Spaniards. There was no way to repay the cost of an expedition; so conquest of the area would be only a waste of time, money, and effort. In addition, Peru with all of its wealth continued to attract more attention than the other South American grants, particularly the Chilean grant. But in spite of Chile's bad reputation and all the deterrents to putting together a successful expedition, there was one man, Pedro de Valdivia, who wanted to conquer Chile.

Valdivia was born between 1498 and 1500 in the province of Extremadura, the birthplace of Almagro and the Pizarros, probably in the town of Villanueva de la Serena. His parents were Pedro Oncas de Melo and Isabel Gutiérrez de Valdivia. Since he took his mother's name, her family probably had a greater reputation than his father's family. When he was about twenty years old, Valdivia entered the army and fought in the Battle of Pavia in 1535 where Francis I of France was captured. Ten years later he went to Venezuela and served there for one year. He then moved on to Peru and fought for Francisco Pizarro against the Almagro faction. As a reward for his services Valdivia persuaded Pizarro to authorize him to conquer and colonize Chile.[11]

In January, 1540, Valdivia led an expedition southward from Cuzco through the Desert of Atacama. After experiencing a difficult journey through the desert and encountering great Indian hostility, Valdivia reached the banks of the Mapocho River. Here he founded Santiago del Nuevo Estremo on February 12, 1541. The Indians placed the newly established town under a siege which lasted almost three years. Within a few months Valdivia learned from captured Indians that Francisco Pizarro had been killed in the Peruvian civil war between the Pizarro and Almagro factions. Since Pizarro had given him authority to conquer Chile, Valdivia was uneasy about his legal right to conquer and colonize Chile. To legalize his position he had the cabildo of Santiago elect him governor in the name of the king, but it was still necessary to have this action approved by a higher authority.

Valdivia obtained recognition of his position seven years later. Toward the end of 1547 he heard of the revolt of Gonzalo Pizarro in Peru. The wrath of Pizarro, like that of most of the Spaniards in the New World,

11

had been aroused by the enforcement of the New Laws, a body of statutes decreed by the Spanish king to prevent abuse of the Indians. Valdivia took ten gentlemen and set sail from Valparaiso, the port of Santiago. In Peru he offered his services to the new governor, Pedro de la Gasca, who appointed him commander of the royal army. Valdivia was able to end the revolt without much bloodshed and to kill Gonzalo Pizarro. As a reward Governor la Gasca formally appointed Valdivia Governor of Chile on April 23, 1548. La Gasca set the boundaries on the north at Copiapó, 27º S., and on the south at 41º S. with an eastern line one hundred leagues inland from the ocean. [12]

Chile as established by the la Gasca grant extended from Copiapó to approximately the present city of Puerto Montt. Although Valdivia petitioned the king to include the Strait of Magellan in his territory, the boundary had not been extended that far by the time he was killed by the Araucanian Indians in January, 1554. Governor Valdivia was successful in extending his jurisdiction across the Andes to Tucumán.

A year after he had confirmed Valdivia Governor of Chile, Pedro de la Gasca authorized Juan Nuñez de Prado to pacify and colonize Tucumán. [13] Nuñez left Peru in 1549 after experiencing trouble with Francisco de Villagra. Villagra, the lieutenant of Valdivia, was recruiting reinforcements for Chile in competition with Nuñez. The two men argued but did not reach the point of blows until they met again in Tucumán in November, 1550. Villagra was on the return trip to Chile when Nuñez attacked him by surprise in the middle of the night. The attacking force was beaten off. The next morning Villagra began pursuit and overtook Nuñez at the newly founded town of Tucumán. The superior force of Villagra compelled Nuñez to recognize the claim of Valdivia. Nuñez also accepted appointment as lieutenant of Valdivia in Tucumán. By this action the boundaries of Chile were extended to include Tucumán.

There followed a period of confusion about jurisdiction over Tucumán until the king settled the question in 1563. The governor of Chile, the Audiencia of Lima, and the viceroy of Peru disputed control of Tucumán. Valdivia was able to continue his control until his death in 1554. He had made provision for continued control from Chile after his death, but the Audiencia of Lima upon learning of the death of Valdivia canceled all appointments made by Valdivia and by the cabildo of Santiago. The Audiencia intended to separate Chile and Tucumán and to make appointments to both. Before the appointments could be made, the viceroy, the Marqués de Cañeta, in 1557 appointed his own son, Garcia Hurtado de Mendoza, interim Governor of Chile with authority over Tucumán. Tucumán remained under Chile until 1563 when Philip II separated Tucumán, Juries, and Diaguitas from the government of Chile and placed them in the district of the Audiencia of Las Charcas. Tucumán was never again included in the boundaries of Chile.

Unlike the attempt to enlarge Chile in the north, expansion southward was more successful. When Jerónimo de Alderate was appointed Governor of Chile in 1555 to succeed Valdivia, the boundaries of Chile were extended south three hundred seventy leagues more or less to the Strait of Magellan.[14] On the same day he was appointed Governor of Chile, he was ordered to explore the Strait area and to send back to Spain information on tides, currents, islands, and customs and habits of the Indians. Governor Alderate was also instructed to take possession of the area, to pacify the natives, and to colonize the territory. Alderate died en route to Chile, and in 1558 Francisco de Villagra, the lieutenant of Valdivia, was named Governor of Chile by the king. The same instructions for the Strait were issued to Governor Villagra.

The cedula naming the new governor was delayed en route three years, and during the interim between 1558 and 1562 García Hurtado de Mendoza acted as governor. Hurtado de Mendoza was responsible for extending the jurisdiction of Chile east across the Andes and for exploration of the Strait of Magellan. In spite of the fact that he was only twenty-two years old, Governor Hurtado de Mendoza founded or refounded towns in the central part of Chile and sent an expedition to Chiloé preparatory to expansion into that area. However, the expedition to Chiloé returned without any notable success and expansion into that region did not develop until later.

The young governor gave command of the Strait expedition to Juan Ladrillero, who sailed with two ships in November, 1557. As they approached the Strait, a storm separated the two vessels sinking one of them. Ladrillero in the remaining ship continued through the Strait and up the southern coast of present-day Argentina. Navigational problems and troubles with the natives delayed the expedition, but after a two-year voyage the survivors returned to Valdivia, the southern Chilean town named after the famous governor, with much useful navigational knowledge and information about the Strait area.

Hurtado de Mendoza enjoyed even greater success in expanding into the transmontane provinces of Chile. One of these provinces was Tucumán, which in 1557 was placed under the leadership of Juan Pérez de Zorita. Pérez de Zorita was appointed lieutenant governor of Tucumán under the authority of Chile. Lieutenant Governor Pérez de Zorita changed the name of the province to Inglaterra and founded three towns, one of which was named Londres. The English names were in honor of Mary of England, who was married to Philip II. In spite of the Chilean activity in this region,

13

the royal cedula of 1563 ended the jurisdiction of Chile over Tucumán.

In the second transmontane province, the province of Cuyo, Chile retained jurisdiction for a longer period of time. Governor Hurtado de Mendoza in November, 1560, appointed Pedro del Castillo lieutenant governor of Cuyo with authority to settle Indian problems and to grant encomiendas. He also expressly forbade Lieutenant Governor Castillo to interfere in any way in Tucumán. In the following weeks Castillo founded the first town in Cuyo and named it Mendoza in honor of the governor of Chile. The jurisdiction of the new town extended from the water divide of the Andes to the Atlantic Ocean. Had these boundaries been accepted in the future, Chile would have obtained the Atlantic as her eastern border.

When Francisco de Villagra replaced Hurtado de Mendoza as governor of Chile in 1562, he appointed Juan Jufré lieutenant governor of Cuyo. The new lieutenant governor expanded settlement northward when he founded the town of San Juan de la Frontera. However, both San Juan and Mendoza remained small and unimportant towns in the colonial period. Toward the end of the colonial period the provinces of Cuyo and San Juan were severed from Chilean jurisdiction.

In the last half of the eighteenth century, Spain and Portugal had trouble over the boundary between their empires in the area of present-day Uruguay. The disagreement reached the point of armed conflict. In order to protect his territories, Charles III prepared to send an army under the command of Pedro de Ceballos. To give Ceballos the prestige and power to meet the Portuguese challenge, Charles III created in 1776 the Viceroyalty of the Río de la Plata and appointed Ceballos the first viceroy.[15] The viceroyalty included Buenos Aires, Paraguay, Tucumán, Potosí, Santa Cruz de la Sierra, Charcas and all of its jurisdiction as well as the provinces of Mendoza and San Juan del Pico, which had formerly been dependencies of Chile. In the following year the viceroyalty was permanently established with the same territories, and the governor of Chile was ordered to refrain from any interference in the territories of the new viceroyalty. At this time Chile lost the last of her transmontane provinces, and the eastern boundary was limited henceforth to the Andes.

Chile was more successful in regaining other territories transferred from her jurisdiction during the last part of the colonial period. Because the Juan Fernández Islands were used by Dutch and English corsairs for refitting and resupplying, the king in 1726 ordered the Viceroy of Peru to assume control of the Islands for security reasons. The Islands were never important nor populated, and Chile was able to assume sovereignty over them after independence with no difficulty.

Another transfer occurred in 1768. The Viceroy of Peru, Manuel

14

de Amat y Junyent Planella Aymerich y Santa Pau, had previously served in Chile and was familiar with the problems of defense in that area. One problem was communications between Santiago and Chiloé. Chiloé was important to the defense of the Strait of Magellan and the control of shipping through the Strait. Viceroy Amat placed Chiloé under the control of his own office because sea communications between Lima and Chiloé were easier than between Santiago and Chiloé. The viceroy was authorized by a general order of the king to make any change necessary for the defense of the Viceroyalty of Peru, and Charles III specifically approved the transfer of Chiloé later the same year.[16] Chiloé remained under the control of the Viceroy of Peru throughout the remainder of the colonial period and was a royalist stronghold during the Revolution. It was not until 1826 that Chile was able to capture Chiloé and again incorporate this area into her territory.

The last of the changes concerned Paposa in the Desert of Atacama between Chile and Peru. Rafael Andreu y Guerrero, Auxiliary Bishop of Charcas, Santiago de Chile, Arequipa, and Córdoba del Tucumán, was in charge of missionary activities among the Indians of these four dioceses. Bishop Andreu requested aid in establishing a missionary settlement at San Nicolás, also called Nuestra Señora del Paposa, and requested ecclesiastical administration for himself. Twenty-two years later, in 1801, the king granted Bishop Andreu's request and placed Paposa under the governor of Chile. Two years later, for security reasons, the king transferred jurisdiction over Paposa and the adjacent coast to the Viceroyalty of Peru. By that time the bishop had lost interest in Paposa and was occupied elsewhere. The area was so unimportant that no one else was interested. Consequently, the Royal Order of 1803 was ignored, and Paposa remained under the jurisdiction of Chile.

A description of the boundaries of Chile during the colonial period shows that her boundaries at the time of independence were loosely defined. In the North, the area adjacent to Paposa was considered the boundary area. Since this area was desert, the lack of a boundary line caused no problem until the discovery of nitrates in the latter half of the nineteenth century. The boundary dispute that followed led to the War of the Pacific before a settlement was reached.

On the east, the Andes were recognized as the boundary when independence was declared. On the northeastern border, Tucumán and Cuyo had been separated from Chile earlier. However, no definite line was drawn, and later a question arose over which range of mountains constituted the boundary. In the South, the boundary ran through an area inhabited almost entirely by Indians. No demarcation was considered necessary

15

until Chile expanded into the Strait of Magellan, giving rise to the question of sovereignty in the Strait and the accompanying dispute over the boundary in the southern Andes.

NOTES

1. Luis Torres de Mendoza, Colección de documentos inéditos, relativos al descubrimiento, conquista y organización de las antiguas posesiones Españoles de America y Oceanía, sacados de los Archivos del Reino, y muy especialmente del Indias, 42 vols. (Madrid: J. M. perez, 1864-1884), 10, pp. 125-132.
2. The cedula is printed in William H. Prescott, Peru, 2 vols. (New York: P. F. Collier & Son, 1901-1902), 2, p. 343.
3. Statement Presented on Behalf of Chile in Reply to the Argentine Report submitted to the Tribunal Constituted by H. B. Majesty's Government acting as Arbitrator in pursuant of the Agreement dated April 17, 1896, 4 vols. (London: Butler & Tanner, 1901-1902), 1, p. 3.
4. Two petitions are printed in Torres de Mendoza, Colección de documentos, 10, pp. 132-133.
5. Marqués de Miraflores and Miguel Salva, Colección de documentos inéditos para la historia de España, 113 vols. (Madrid: Vidua de Calvo, 1842-1895), 68, pp. 206-208.
6. Torres de Mendoza, Colección de documentos, 22, pp. 338, 350, 360.
7. Alcazaba left no journal. An eyewitness account of the voyage is Alonso (Veedor), "Narrative of the Events which Happened in the Fleet of Simon Alcazaba who went out as Governor of the Province of Leon in the Parts of the South Seas. Having to Pass the Strait of Magellan. He took two ships, the Capitana called Madre de Dios and the Other called San Pedro in which were embarked, including passengers and sailors, 250 persons," Early Spanish Voyages to the Strait of Magellan, Trans. Clements Markham, The Hakluyt Society Publications, Series 2, vol. 28 (London: 1911).
8. Pedro Sarmiento de Gamboa, Viajes al Estrecho de Magallanes, 1579-1584, Recopilación de sus relaciones sobre los dos viajes al Estrecho y de sus cartas y memoriales con un apéndice documental sobre su vida y sus viajes, ed. Ángel Rosenblat, 2 vols. (Buenos Aires: Emecé Editores, 1950).

16

9. Ulrich Schmidt, "A true and agreeable description of some principal Indian lands and islands, which have not been recorded in former Chronicles, but have now been first explored amid great danger during the voyages of Ulrich Schmidt von Straubingen, and most-carefully described by him, " The Conquest of the River Plate (1535-1555), trans. Luis L. Domingues, The Hakluyt Society Publications, no. 81 (London: 1891).

10. Diego Barros Arana, Historia jeneral de Chile, 16 vols. (Santiago: R. Jover, 1884-1902), 1, p. 158, footnote 13. Enrique de Gandia, Historia de la conquista del Río de la Plata y del Paraguay. Los Gobiernos de Don Pedro de Mendoza, Alvar Nuñez y Domingo de Irala 1535-1556 (Buenos Aires: A. Garcia Santos, 1932), p. 13.

11. José Toribio Medina, Cartas de Pedro de Valdivia que tratan del descubrimiento y conquista de Chile (Sevilla: M. Carmons, 1924).

12. Miraflores and Salva, Colección de documentos de España, 2, p. 387.

13. Ricardo Jaime Freyre, El Tucumán colonial documentos y mapas del Archivo de Indias (Buenos Aires: Coni Aermanos, 1915). Roberto Levillier, Nueva crónica de la conquista del Tucumán, 3 vols. (Buenos Aires: Editorial Nosotros, 1926-1930), 1. Manuel Lizondo Borda, Historia de la Gobernación del Tucumán (Siglo XVI) (Buenos Aires: Coni, 1928).

14. The cedulas of this period relating to Tucumán and Cuyo may be found in Medina, Colección de documentos, 23.

15. Javier Vial Solar, Los tratados de Chile, 2 vols. (Santiago: Barcelona, 1903), 1, pp. 315-320.

16. See Vicente Rodriguez Casedo and Florentino Perez Embid, Construcciones Militares del Virrey Amat (Sevilla: Escuela de Estudios Hispano-americanos-Alfonso XII, 1949). Vial Solar, Tratados de Chile, 1.

CHAPTER 2. INDEPENDENCE AND THE
FIRST YEARS OF THE REPUBLIC

EVENTS occurring outside the colony precipitated the independence movement in the Captaincy General of Chile. In August, 1808, the news of the Napoleonic invasion of Spain reached Santiago, and a little later the fate of Charles IV and of Ferdinand VII became known. Napoleon conferred with the Spanish royal family at Bayonne, France, and persuaded the two Bourbon kings to abdicate the throne. Napoleon, then, placed his oldest brother, Joseph, on the Spanish throne. The Chileans refused to recognize Joseph as their sovereign and continued to give their allegiance to Ferdinand, who remained at Valencay, France, for six years as the guest of Napoleon. Charles had little support in Spain or the Spanish Empire and retired to Rome. Since the king was the only link between the mother country and the colonies, confusion resulted. In this period of confusion the independence movement grew.

The situation in Chile was further complicated by the death of Governor Luis Muñoz Guzmán in February, 1808. Provision had been made for this kind of situation, but the attempt by the Audiencia of Santiago to ignore the legally established procedures caused problems. The Royal Order of October 23, 1806, provided for such cases by naming the highest ranking officer holding the rank of colonel or brigadier the interim governor. The Audiencia of Santiago attempted unsuccessfully to appoint its oldest member interim governor in violation of the Royal Order. Objections to this move led to the appointment of Brigadier Pedro Quijada, the ranking officer. Because of his age, seventy-four, and ill health, he refused the position. Then the second ranking officer, Brigadier Francisco Antonio García Carresco, was appointed.

Governor García Carresco was a military man with no social position, no governmental experience, and little education. He lacked tact and did not have the confidence of the aristocratic element of the colony. These people resented a person of low social status holding the highest social and political position in Chile. Under these circumstances Governor García

Carresco would have had difficulty gaining acceptance even if his administration had not been initiated with a blunder. García Carresco illegally extended the term of the rector of the royal university at Santiago. The faculty was so opposed that the governor was forced to approve the election of a new rector. In the election the most outspoken critic of the governor, Father Vicente Martinez de Aldunate of Santa Ana parish in Santiago, was chosen by the faculty as the new rector. Santiago celebrated the election victory with a fiesta and illumination of the streets at night, the same celebration as that used for a great military victory. Such complete success in the first encounter with the new governor encouraged further resistance, and García Carresco was unwilling to learn from his first experience in office.

As conditions became more confused in Spain and in Chile, Governor García Carresco became more arbitrary and reactionary. He remained loyal to Ferdinand VII and obeyed the instructions of the Junta of Seville, which had been established after the abdication of the Bourbons to act in the name of Ferdinand VII. Most Chileans remained loyal to the king, but the governor exaggerated any opposition. The two major groups opposing loyalty to Ferdinand were the Carlotistas and the Bonapartists. Princess Carlota, the daughter of Charles IV and sister of Ferdinand VII, was the wife of Prince John, Regent of Portugal. The Portuguese royal family had fled to Brazil to avoid capture by Napoleon, the fate of the Spanish Bourbons. Once in Brazil, Princess Carlota attempted to gain support in the Spanish colonies for an independent Bourbon empire in the New World with herself as monarch. There were also suggestions that Princess Carlota should act as regent for her brother until he was free to resume the throne himself. The second group, the Bonapartists, followed the example of some of the highest nobility of Spain. As Napoleon became more and more successful in overrunning Spain, they decided to accept Joseph as king and no longer resisted the French. Neither group received much support in Chile or other parts of the Spanish Empire. However, Governor Carcía Carresco saw sedition and treason throughout Chile.

In order to control the situation, the governor prohibited any discussion of events in Spain and expelled all foreigners living in the Captaincy General. He also insulted the cabildo, delayed the election by the cabildo of the Chilean delegates to the Cortes at Cadiz, and suspended officials who displeased him in any way. The fact that the cabildo was composed of creoles favoring autonomy or in a few instances even independence made relations between the governor and that group understandably strained, but the governor's inability to get along with the royal audiencia, the stronghold of royalism in Chile, is a good measure of the governor's unpopularity. At times even the audiencia was antagonized by the governor and opposed his arbitrary and reactionary measures.

By 1810 the situation in Chile was so tense that any incident could cause a reaction. The governor provided this incident when, in May, 1810, he took action against three creoles who were prominent members of the Chilean aristocracy. García Carresco suspected Juan Antonio Ovalle, José Antonio Rojas, and Bernardo Vera of subversive activities. One night he suddenly and arbitrarily arrested them, had their homes searched, and ordered them deported to Peru. That same night, before any resistance could be organized, the governor sent the three prisoners to Valparaiso for transfer to Peru as soon as a ship was available. The news of this arbitrary action soon spread over Santiago and enraged the creoles. Encouraged by the unwillingness of the troops to maintain order, the citizens demonstrated in the streets. Because of the unrest and the lack of proof against the three prisoners, Governor García Carresco publicly rescinded the arrest order and assured the people that no action would be taken against the men. Secretly, the governor ordered the deportation to be carried out, taking care that no news of the action would be leaked to the public. He wanted to avoid another disturbance in the streets. When his act became known, such a vehement protest developed that García Carresco was persuaded to resign in favor of Mateo de Toro Zambrano, Conde de la Conquista.

The Conde de la Conquista was a native-born member of the Chilean aristocracy. He was legally qualified for office since he had been appointed brigadier general the year before by the Central Junta in Spain. Because he was in his seventies and had not participated in the opposition to Governor García Carresco, both the royalists in the audiencia and the patriots in the cabildo believed that they could influence his decisions. As events developed, the patriots in the cabildo were more successful.

In spite of royalist opposition in the audiencia, the patriots were able to persuade the Conde de la Conquista to call a cabildo abierto, a meeting of the cabildo to which members of the various social, economic, and religious organizations known as the corporations were invited. The precedent for such action had been established by the Central Junta in Spain. The stated purpose of the cabildo abierto was to form a junta to conduct the government of the Captaincy General while the king was held captive. The real purpose was to introduce self-government. In the plans of some of the patriots in the cabildo, this was the first step toward independence. The cabildo abierto met on September 18, 1810. At this meeting the Conde de la Conquista surrendered the staff of office, the symbol of executive authority in Chile, to the cabildo abierto.

20

The cabildo abierto then elected members to the junta which would function as a provisional government until elections in the whole Captaincy General could be held. The patriots in the cabildo had previously chosen a slate of candidates and had also arranged support for them. Included in this slate were the Conde de la Conquista for president; the bishop-elect of Santiago, José Antonio Martinez de Aldunate, for vice-president; and three additional members, Fernando Marques de la Plata, Juan Martinez de Rozas, and Ignacio de la Carrera. The royalist could not prevent the election by acclamation of the slate, but they did succeed in adding two royalist to the junta, Colonel Francisco Javier de Reina and Juan Enrique Rosales.

The seven member junta permitted the cabildo of Santiago to determine the number of deputies each department would have in the congress and the method of holding elections. This congress, elected by all of the departments, would decide the form of government and choose the leaders. Santiago, of course, received a disproportionately large representation, and the other departments resented domination by Santiago.

The newly elected congress chose July 4, 1811, for the opening session in honor of the thirty-fifth anniversary of the Declaration of Independence of the United States of America. This congress proclaimed loyalty to Ferdinand VII and claimed to rule in his name. Initially very little else was accomplished. The congress's failure to distinguish between executive and legislative responsibilities resulted in confusion and inefficiency. To remedy the situation, an executive council subordinate to the congress was established.

The Provisional Executive Authority of Chile was created by the so-called Constitution of 1811. This act of August 8, 1811, can be more accurately described as a law delegating executive powers to a council that would function under the supervision of congress.[1] Little power was actually delegated to the council. Congress reserved for itself the right to intervene and control executive actions. The Constitution of 1811 was concerned solely with the creation of the Provisional Executive Authority and did not mention legislative or judicial powers. Boundaries were also ignored in this constitution.

Complete dependence upon a congress jealous of its authority and torn by factional strife made it impossible for the weak executive council to direct successfully any program of national action. In congress the conservatives, the radicals, and the reform groups could not cooperate at all. Consequently, little could be accomplished by either the Congress or the Provisional Executive Authority. When improvement programs offered by the radicals and the reformists, who leaned toward the radical point of view, were completely frustrated by congressional division and executive inaction, dissatisfaction among the radicals grew.

This growing dissatisfaction was used by one of the radical leaders, José Miguel Carrera, to gain support for a change he desired in the membership of the junta. After a show of force, Carrera and his radical group took control of the junta and on September 4, 1811, reorganized it to include Juan Enrique Rosales, Juan Martinez de Rozas, Martin Calvo Encalada, Juan MacKenna, and Gaspar Marin. In order to reduce the disproportionate representation of Santiago and to decrease the conservative element in Congress, eight delegates, six of whom were from Santiago, were dropped. This arrangement lasted until November when another show of force permitted José Miguel Carrera to reorganize the government again. Now the junta was reduced to three members, one representing each of the three provinces in the colonial administrative structure. José Miguel Carrera represented Santiago; Gaspar Marin represented Coquimbo; and Juan Martinez de Rozas represented Concepción. Because Martinez de Rozas was in Concepción and not expected to return to Santiago, Bernardo O'Higgins was selected as the substitute for him. The second junta lasted about two weeks.

In the first days of December, 1811, Carrera assumed complete control of the government. At the same time he detained the legislature by force until the members signed a document voluntarily surrendering their powers to the executive junta. By eight o'clock in the evening the signatures were obtained, and the deputies were released but not permitted to leave Santiago. Gaspar Marin and Bernardo O'Higgins resigned from the executive junta in protest. Marin was permitted to return to Coquimbo, but O'Higgins, who posed a military threat to Carrera, was detained in Santiago. José Miguel Carrera with his two brothers, Luis and Juan José, controlled the government and army in Santiago. Outside Santiago Martinez de Rozas was the most powerful opponent of the Carreras, and he fell from power in Concepción in July of the following year.

In August, 1812, work began on a new constitution that was promulgated in October. [2] Included in the preamble was an explanation of the conditions in Spain and Spanish America that made it necessary for Chile to establish her own government. The same explanation also recognized the fact that a permanent government could not be created at that time. This constitution, therefore, was designed to establish a temporary government which could be changed later by delegates chosen to set up a permanent government.

The temporary Constitution of 1812 recognized the sovereignty of Ferdinand VII and established a Supreme Governing Board composed of three members and two secretaries. The board ruled as the representative of the king. A senate of seven members and the cabildo, which by that time was popularly elected, formed the legislative branch of the government. Judicial powers remained with the existing courts and magistrates. Also incorporated was a bill of rights that included inviolability of the person and his property, freedom of the press, equality before the law, and due process of law for all; but the guarantees of personal liberty and freedom were not observed by Carrera after the constitution went into effect. The constitution did not guarantee political rights for all citizens or even define citizenship. The Apostolic Catholic Religion was established. but the omission of the word Roman drew opposition from the Church. Since no statement of boundaries or definition of national territory was included, the area over which the government would exercise control remained indefinite.

After promulgation of the constitution, Carrera was faced with a civil war as well as a royalist invasion directed by the viceroy of Peru. In the South the Peruvian dependency of Chiloé and the Chilean city of Valdivia were royalist strongholds. It was into this area that Viceroy Fernando de Abascal sent expeditions for the reconquest of Chile. Ancud on Chiloé and Valdivia became the bases of operations for the royalist armies. The task of the royalist armies was made easier by the dispute between Santiago and Concepción. The Carrera brothers, who constituted the highest political and military leadership of the patriot forces in central Chile, at times even quarrelled among themselves, but the Carrera's fear and jealousy of two successful patriot generals, Juan Mackenna and Bernardo O'Higgins. made it possible for them to unite against their enemies, patriot or royalist.

In spite of internal dissension, the patriot forces were able to contain the royalist army and even make some advances until the winter (July and August) of 1813. Then, the fortunes of war turned in favor of the royalists, and both sides resorted to very cruel warfare. In March, 1814. José Miguel and Luis Carrera were captured by the royalists at the fall of Talca. To replace José Miguel Carrera, Francisco de la Lastra was named Supreme Director.

To legalize the new government a new constitution was written by a constitutional committee composed of Francisco Antonio Pérez, Camilo Henríquez, José María Rozas, Andrés Nicolás de Orjera, and José Antonio Errázuriz. An assembly of representatives of the corporations approved the constitution which was promulgated by Supreme Director Lastra in mid March, 1814. [3] The new government was composed of an executive with broad powers called the Supreme Director and a consultative senate of seven members who were selected by the Supreme Director

23

from a list of twenty-one names chosen by the council of corporations.

The uncertainty of the war made a powerful central government firmly controlled by a strong president seem necessary. Chileans were willing to accept this conservative governmental system because of the military defeats suffered by the patriot army. In fact, this new government was similar to that of the colonial period; the powers of the Supreme Director were as extensive as those of the Captain General, and the function of the consultative senate was much the same as that of the audiencia. The constitution made no mention of judicial functions, citizenship, the exercise of political rights, sovereignty of the government, or boundaries. These omissions can be explained by the unstable nature of a government threatened with reconquest by the royalist.

In April Supreme Director Lastra and the royalist commander, Gabino Gaínza, concluded the Treaty of Lircay, which provided for the cessation of hostilities, exchange of prisoners, and evacuation of the royalist army. Chile agreed to recognize the sovereignty of Ferdinand VII and to elect delegates to the Spanish Cortes. A secret clause of the treaty permitted the royalists to continue to detain the Carrera brothers. The patriots agreed to the detention because they recognized the Carreras as a potential threat to unity within their cause, but General Gaínza knew why the patriots agreed and permitted the Carreras to escape. As General Gaínza had anticipated, José Miguel Carrera returned to Santiago and again assumed power. Fighting among the patriots broke out.

The viceroy of Peru disavowed the Treaty of Lircay and sent a new army under the command of General Mariano Osorio to subdue Chile. In the face of the new threat, the patriots declared a truce among themselves and agreed to cooperate to defeat the royalists. Jealousies and distrust prevailed instead. When a patriot army under the command of O'Higgins met the royalist army at the Battle of Rancagua on October 1, 1814, José Miguel Carrera withheld his army and refused to go to the aid of O'Higgins. The patriot army was crushed. All of the patriots were forced to flee across the Andes to Mendoza, Argentina. The more moderate faction of the patriots blamed José Miguel Carrera for the defeat and never forgave him.

From the Battle of Rancagua in 1814 to José de San Martín's passage of the Andes in 1817, the royalists ruled Chile. General Osorio and his successor Francisco Casimiro Marcó del Pont alienated many Chileans by their reactionary policies and dictatorial methods. The patriot cause became more and more popular. Thus, the royalists leaders paved the way for the successful conclusion of the independence movement in Chile.

Chilean independence was achieved as the result of the cooperative efforts of José de San Martín and Bernardo O'Higgins. The Army of the Andes was created by San Martín in Mendoza, the capital of the Argentine province of Cuyo. Cuyo, located across the Andes from Santiago, was the former transmontane province of Chile transferred to Argentina in 1776. When the Chilean exiles of 1814 fled across the Andes, they joined the army of San Martín, who was one of the few successful generals in the Argentine liberation movement. Included among the exiles was O'Higgins, whom San Martín appointed his lieutenant. San Martín realized that Argentina could not be secure in her independence until Peru was no longer a stronghold from which royalist attacks could be launched. He planned the liberation of Chile as the first step in the liberation of Peru. With Chile as a base, a seaborne invasion would free Peru and assure independence for Argentina as well as Chile.

In the middle of summer, on January 9, 1817, San Martín with the assistance of O'Higgins led his army across the Andes through the Uspallata and Los Patos passes to Chile. In mid April General Osorio was defeated, ensuring the independence of Chile. The cabildo of Santiago offered San Martín the position of Supreme Director of Chile. Because of his plans for the liberation of Peru, San Martín refused the honor and recommended O'Higgins for the office. The cabildo then offered the position to O'Higgins. O'Higgins accepted and organized a new government. The following year another constitution was written to legalize the O'Higgins government. [4] This constitution established a strong, centralized government under the control of the Supreme Director. Chile was divided into three provinces, La Capital, Coquimbo, and Concepción; but there were no boundaries stated for the provinces or for the nation.

During the five years the Constitution of 1818 was in force, O'Higgins as Supreme Director ruled Chile in a dictatorial manner. He abolished titles of nobility and coats of arms, granted concessions to foreign nationals, and antagonized a large segment of the clergy and the faithful by exiling the royalist Bishop of Santiago, prohibiting burials in the churches, and permitting burial of non-Catholics in cemeteries. His popularity was further reduced when he abolished bullfights and cockfights and attempted to suppress gambling and alcoholism.

To placate the growing number of discontented Chileans, O'Higgins granted a constitution which seemed more democratic. [5] The second constitution promulgated by the O'Higgins government was the work of José Antonio Rodriguez Aldea, Minister of Finance and later Minister of War. Rodriguez Aldea was a former royalist who had changed to the patriot cause only a few years before O'Higgins appointed him to high office in his government. Patriots of longstanding resented the favor shown Rodriguez by

25

O'Higgins. Nevertheless, O'Higgins kept the minister in office because they both believed that Chile was not yet ready for democracy. Both men believed the country needed a paternalistic government directed by a strong man.

The Constitution of 1822 was a combination of the Spanish Constitution of 1812 and the Chilean Constitution of 1818. An attempt was made to hide its autocractic features by using democratic language and resorting to a deliberate lack of organization in the document. Few people were deceived; the constitution did not satisfy the opposition factions. By the end of the year O'Higgins was overthrown and the constitution discarded.

The Constitution of 1822 included the first statement of territorial limits for the country. Article three of chapter one defines the boundaries as Cape Horn on the south, the Desert of Atacama on the north, the Andes on the east, and the Pacific Ocean on the west. The islands of the Archipelago of Chiloé and the islands of la Mocha, Juan Fernández, and Santa María groups as well as other adjacent islands are included in the territory of Chile. [6] The first boundary description in the independence period is stated in terms of areas as was characteristic of the colonial period. This method of describing boundaries became the model for succeeding constitutions.

When General Ramón Freire succeeded O'Higgins as Supreme Director in 1823, a new constitution was written. Juan Egaña was the chief author, and the new constitution reflects his belief in a highly centralized government with no separation of executive and legislative powers. The Supreme Director, relying upon the rich and the wellborn for support, was once again the most powerful figure in the government. This constitution remained in effect only six months before it too was discarded.

The Egaña constitution defined the national boundaries in almost the same manner as the 1823 constitution, from Cape Horn to the Desert of Atacama and from the Cordillera of the Andes to the Pacific Ocean with all the adjacent islands including those named the year before. [7] The term cordillera, first introduced in the Egaña constitution, became important later in the settlement of the Chilean-Argentine boundary.

Although the Constitution of 1823 was suspended in July of the same year, it was not annulled until January, 1825. The years between 1823 and 1828 are known as the period of chaos and anarchy. General Freire was able to maintain his postion as Supreme Director because he retained control of the army. His power did not extend beyond foreign affairs; internal affairs were in the hands of the individual provinces. Federalism existed in fact but not in the constitution. In 1826 Supreme Director Freire issued a call for a constitutional assembly. However, before the assem-

26

bly met, Freire resigned as Supreme Director, but he retained command of the armed forces.

The political thinking of the constitutional assembly of 1826 was predominantly federal. The chief exponent of federalism in Chile, José Miguel Infante, led the assembly in writing a liberal, federal document that was never promulgated. Instead, a series of laws passed between July, 1826, and February, 1827, set up a federal regime in which a president and vice-president replaced the supreme director.[8] Manuel Blanco Encalada, the first admiral of the national fleet and a member of the aristocracy, was elected president by the assembly to serve until the constitution went into effect. Nearly all of the other officers of the national government as well as of the local governments became elective. Even parish priests became elected officials. Elective provincial legislatures and governors made federalism an actuality.

Because a series of laws rather than a constitution formed the basis of government, no statement of national boundaries was given. However, eight provinces were established, and boundaries for them were described. The northernmost province, Coquimbo, had the Desert of Atacama as its northern limit. In the South the province of Valdivia included all of the territory granted to Pedro de Valdivia, and the province of Chiloé included all of the Archipelago of Chiloé. Eastern and western boundaries were stated for only one province, Aconcagua, immediately south of Coquimbo. The Andes on the east and the Pacific Ocean on the west constituted the Aconcagua boundaries. These general statements cannot be regarded as official boundary descriptions, but they do tell us what the members of the assembly regarded as the general extent of the national territory.

The 1826 arrangement of basing the government on laws instead of a constitution was intended to be in effect only until a new constitution could be promulgated, but conditions became so confused that it was impossible to get a constitution written. No one retained executive power for very long. Revolts among the Indians and in the army occurred regularly; local governing bodies refused to acknowledge any superior power, and taxes went unpaid. A national government could not and did not exist.

Finally, in June of 1827, General Francisco Antonio Pinto, vice-president under General Freire and acting president after Freire's resignation, persuaded Congress to call elections for a new constitutional convention and then dissolve. In this convention, which met in February, 1828, a majority of the delegates were pipioles favoring federalism. The liberal, federal document approved in August was the work of José Joaquin de Mora, an exiled Spanish liberal. A more popular government was established with broad suffrage and a bill of rights. The executive power was

27

limited.

The description of the boundaries included in the Constitution of 1828 was very similar to the one in the Constitution of 1823: from the Desert of Atacama on the north to Cape Horn on the south, from the Cordillera of the Andes to the Pacific Ocean, and the Islands of Juan Fernández and the other adjacent ones. [9] Although la Mocha, Santa María, and the Archipelago of Chiloé are not specifically mentioned, they are included in the phrase, "the other adjacent ones."

The Constitution of 1828 like its predecessors was destined for a short life. In the elections that had been established by this constitution many irregularities occurred. The conservatives who lost the elections declared them null. Then a more important event took place. General Pinto, a liberal, was elected chief executive, but no candidate for vice-president received a majority of the electoral votes. Congress, exercising its constitutional powers, met to elect the vice-president. Since the two candidates with the largest number of votes were conservatives, Congress, dominated by liberals, chose a third candidate, who was liberal. The conservatives rejected the election as unconstitutional and revolted in favor of General Joaquin Prieto, one of the defeated vice-presidential candidates. At the Battle of Lircay on April 17, 1830, General Prieto decisively defeated the liberals. The following year the General assumed the presidency and established a conservative government.

The dominant political figure in the Prieto government was Diego Portales, a member of one of Chile's leading commercial families. Under his direction the government of 1830 was reorganized for efficiency and unity. The army was subordinated to civilian officials, and officers who had participated in rebellions were mustered out. Law and order were restored, and the leading opponents of the government were exiled. Portales achieved a stable, civilian government based upon dictatorial power and supported by the conservative, aristocratic element and the Church.

President Prieto had been in office about two years when Congress called a constitutional convention to amend the 1828 constitution. Although Congress had limited the convention to revising the old constitution, the convention, after meeting for two years, finally drafted an entirely new constitution. The new constitution was promulgated on May 25, 1833. The aristocracy, which already dominated economically and socially, now dominated politically as well. Stability and law and order were the primary concerns of the framers of this document. These aims were achieved, and the Constitution of 1833 became the fundamental law of Chile until 1926.

The government established by this constitution consisted of a president assisted by a three man council appointed by the president, a bicam-

28

eral legislature, and the judicial system already in existence. The lower house of congress was elected by direct popular vote; the upper house and president were elected indirectly. The conservative composition of the upper house was assured by a constitutional provision that each member must have an income of 20,000 pesos a year. This conservative upper house elected the permanent legislative commission, which acted for congress when it was not in session. The president had extensive appointive powers, a veto over legislation, and authority to declare martial law in any part of the republic. Suffrage was limited to male citizens, twenty-five years of age if single or twenty-one if married, who possessed property or capital in an amount to be determined by each province every ten years. These restrictions limited suffrage to the small portion of the population that was conservative.

The first article of the constitution contained a geographic description of the nation much like those in preceding constitutions. "The territory of Chile extends from the Desert of Atacama to Cape Horn, and from the Cordillera of the Andes to the Pacicfic Ocean, including the Archipelago of Chiloé, all the adjacent islands, and those of Juan Fernández."[10] This constitution remained in force throughout the period of dispute and determination of the Chilean boundaries.

The Great Convention had a twofold purpose in including a general statement of national territory. The first was to prevent any European nation or combination of European nations from attempting to reconquer or to exercise sovereignty over any portion of Chile. The second was to prevent boundary disputes in the future by giving the nations of the world a constitutional statement of the sovereign area of Chile. The statement in the constitutional accomplished neither of these purposes. Although Chile, after independence, was never threatened with conquest by any European nation, the boundary definition in the constitution was not responsible. The second objective was no more successful since Chile has had boundary disputes with all three neighboring countries with whom she has common boundaries.

The islands mentioned in the various constitutions consist of two general groups, those situated near the coast and those lying a considerable distance from the mainland. In the first group, the islands of the southern archipelagos and the Island of Chiloé were not involved in boundary disputes. Although administrative control of the island had been transferred to the Viceroyalty of Peru for a time in the middle of the eighteenth century, Chiloé had always been considered a part of the Kingdom of Chile during the colonial period and remained part of the national territory after independence. The islands of the archipelagos were unsuitable for colonization and had no products to attract exploitation. No nation objected or even noticed when Chile proclaimed sovereignty over this southern region in the mid nineteenth century.

La Mocha and Santa María also belong to the coastal islands group. Santa María lies about three miles off the northern coast of the province of Arauco, and la Mocha is twenty and one-half miles off the southern coast of the same province. Santa María is situated about two hundred fifty miles and la Mocha about four hundred miles south of Valparaiso. Both islands have been under the jurisdiction of Chile since independence. No other nation has ever advanced a claim to the islands or even shown any interest in them.

Included in the islands farther from the Chilean coast are Easter, San Ambrosio, and the Juan Fernández. Easter Island, Isla de Pascua, or Rapa Nui is the outermost island. It is situated about 2,300 miles west of the coast of Atacama and was formerly included in the jurisdiction of that province. The island is triangularly shaped, about fifteen miles long and eleven miles wide. It was discovered by the Dutchman Jacob Roggeveen on Easter Day, 1722, hence the name.[11] Chile proclaimed sovereignty over the island in 1888. Because Easter Island is small, unimportant, and isolated, no nation has seriously disputed Chilean sovereignty. In 1895 the Chilean government leased the island to a commercial company for sheep raising, and the island gained some commercial value, exporting wool and hides. Living conditions on the island do not attract immigrants, and the small population has remained stationary in recent years. Actually there is little to interest people except the large, unique, stone statues found there. To preserve these and other remains of the native culture, Easter Island became a national park in 1935. It is now protected from destruction and commercial exploitation. However, the number of visitors is small and because of the isolated location seems unlikely to increase.

Both the Juan Fernández Islands and the San Ambrosio Islands were discovered by the Spanish Captain Juan Fernández in 1574. Little is known about the early life of Captain Fernández. There is some confusion because four men in Peru had this name, and it is not always possible to know to which Juan Fernández the documents refer.[12] Captain Fernández had sailed between Peru and Chile before 1574 and knew the difficulties of the voyage. The trip between Chile and Peru with favorable winds and currents was usually a month or two long. The southbound trip seldom took less than four to six months and was particularly difficult because of the lack of fresh water along the shore and unfavorable winds and currents. It was during a search for an easier sea route between Callao and Valparaiso that Juan Fernández discovered both island groups.

In October, 1574, Captain Fernández sailed from Callao on a voyage to Chile. Instead of following the coast as was the custom, he set out to sea to avoid the winds and currents from the south. On the eleventh day of the voyage, November 6, an island was sighted and named San Felix for the Saint's Day upon which the journey had started. San Ambor or San Ambrosio was also sighted at this time. Two more islands were discovered on November 22 and named Santa Cecilia. Today these two are part of the Juan Fernández Islands. The voyage ended at Valparaiso on November 25, thirty days after sailing from Callao. The discovery of this new, fast sea route between Callao and Valparaiso greatly benefited Chile. The new route considerably increased Chile's commercial activity.

The Juan Fernández Islands, which were part of the province of Valparaiso during the nineteenth and early part of the twentieth centuries, consist of three islands: Mas a Tierra. Mas a Fuera, and Santa Clara. The largest and most important is Mas a Tierra, located about four hundred miles west of Valparaiso. The island was important to Spanish colonial authorities because it was used as a port of supply by corsairs operating along the Pacific coast of South America. Both the viceroy of Peru and the captain general of Chile were interested in controlling the island, and during the colonial period each exercised authority at different times. In this same period the English sailor Alexander Selkirk was marooned there from 1704 to 1709. Selkirk's experience probably served as the basis for Daniel Defoe's Robinson Crusoe. During the revolutionary period Mas a Tierra became a prison for Chilean patriots captured by the royalists. The Chilean government continued to use the island as a prison for several years after independence. In the twentieth century some economic development occurred when lobster fishing by the islanders was permitted. The Juan Fernández Islands and the Territory of Magellan are the only lobster fishing areas in Chile.

Mas a Fuera, the second largest island in the Juan Fernández group, is also called Isla de los Perros because of the wild, savage dogs which at one time inhabited it. It is located one hundred miles west of Mas a Tierra. The island has less than one hundred inhabitants and is of no great importance.

The third island is Santa Clara, one and one-half miles off the southwestern tip of Mas a Tierra. This island is arid and difficult to approach because of the heavy surf which breaks almost constantly on the shores. Santa Clara is uninhabited and has no value for commerce or colonization. The Juan Fernández Islands were made a national park and colonization or exploitation of the flora or fauna was prohibited by the same decree that made Easter Island a national park.

31

San Ambrosio and San Felix are small, arid, and uninhabited islands. They are included in the province of Atacama and are located about five hundred miles off the coast of that province. The two islands are approximately ten miles apart with San Felix in the westernmost position. The surrounding waters provide excellent fishing, the only valuable asset of the islands. Because of their limited value, Chile has experienced no problems exercising sovereignty over these islands.

NOTES

1. Ricardo Anguita, Leyes promulgada en Chile desde 1810 hasta el 1 de junio de 1912 (Santiago: Imprenta, Litografía i Encuadernación Barcelona, 1912), pp. 26-27.
2. Anguita, Leyes, pp. 31-33.
3. Anguita, Leyes, p. 42.
4. Anguita, Leyes, pp. 51-59.
5. Paul V. Shaw, The Early Constitutions of Chile, 1810-1833 (New York: F. Mayana, 1930), pp. 90-91.
6. Anguita, Leyes, p. 102.
7. Anguita, Leyes, p. 127.
8. Anguita, Leyes, pp. 167-177.
9. Anguita, Leyes, pp. 180-181.
10. Anguita, Leyes, p. 215.
11. Bolton Glanvill Corney, ed., The Voyages of Captain Don Felipe Gonzalez in the Ship of the Line San Lorenzo, with the Frigate Santa Rosalita in Company, to Easter Island in 1770-1: Preceded by an Extract from Mynheer Jacob Roggeveen's Official Log of his Discovery of and visit to Easter Island in 1772 (Cambridge: John Clay, 1908), Hakluyt Society Publications, Second Series, no. 13.
12. For a discussion see José Toribio Medina, El piloto Juan Fernández descubridor de las islas que llevan su nombre y Juan Jufré armador de la expedición que hizo en busca de otras en el Mar del Sur: estudio historico (Santiago: Imprenta Elzeviriana, 1943), ch. 1.

CHAPTER 3. THE NORTHERN BOUNDARY

FROM the beginning of the Independence Movement in 1810 to the
mid 1830's, Chile was concerned with her internal problems and with establishing a stable government. Diego Portales with the support of the
Church and the conservative landowning and commercial classes had just
achieved such a government when trouble between Chile and the Peruvian-
Bolivian Confederation developed. Chile was unwilling to permit the union
of her two northern neighbors. In her eyes such a confederation would
create a threat to Chilean national existence. In 1836 war broke out between Chile and the two northern nations and continued for three years. It
was not until 1840 that Chile was able to turn her attention to her boundaries. By that time Chile had cause for concern.

Prior to 1840 two events of importance to future boundary disputes
had occurred. The first one, the surveying voyages of the English ships
Adventure and Beagle between 1826 and 1836, led to the southern boundary
problem with Argentina. The other, the discovery of nitrates in the Desert of Atacama, resulted in the dispute over the northern boundary.

The northern desert, which became the center of a boundary dispute between Chile and Bolivia, was explored for mineral resources as
early as the 1830's. The discovery of a few deposits of copper and silver
that could be profitably mined encouraged further exploration. During
the decade of the 1840's Chile expanded to the north and to the south, colonizing the Strait of Magellan and expanding into the northern desert in
search of minerals. At this time Peru and Bolivia began to ship large
amounts of nitrates to Europe for use as fertilizer. The European markets provided profits for the nitrate companies, and an export tax provided
revenues for Peru and Bolivia. Not until the last part of the 1850's were
nitrates discovered in the southern portion of the Desert of Atacama. Part
of the area was under Bolivian sovereignty, and part was disputed by Bolivia
and Chile. Chilean capital dominated in the development of the southern
area, and a majority of the laborers in the nitrate works in both regions
were Chilean. The desert had become valuable to both private enterprise

and government.

Prior to the discovery of nitrate deposits, Chile and Bolivia had disagreed upon their boundary. The boundary question dated back to the independence period, but internal problems as well as the fact that the boundary was located in a desert that had no value at that time caused the dispute to be forgotten or ignored. Nitrates revived the dispute and increased the difficulties of peacefully settling the boundary.

In 1842 large deposits of guano were discovered in Peru, and although guano was not yet a great source of income, its importance was recognized. The government of Chile sent an expedition to find guano in that portion of the Desert of Atacama under its sovereignty, the area up to the twenty-third parallel at Mejillones. A few small deposits were found but not sufficient amounts to warrant exploitation. Nevertheless, President Manuel Bulnes sent a message to Congress requesting nationalization of guano deposits in the national territory from the twenty-third parallel south. Congress responded on October 31, 1842, by nationalizing all guano deposits from the Bay of Mejillones southward.[1] Congress also authorized the president to collect an export tax on guano and made all ships illegally loading guano subject to seizure.

Bolivia protested that her southern border was the twenty-sixth parallel not the twenty-third as Chile had stated in this legislation. The three degrees between 23º and 26º S., an area about two hundred miles long, became the disputed territory. From 1842 to 1863 jurisdictional controversies in the disputed region occurred with increasing frequency.[2] Neither country would recognize the mineral concessions granted by the other. Both governments seized vessels loading guano under the authority of the other and attempted to collect the export tax. Because of the increasing difficulties and the importance of guano revenues, the situation could not continue.

During this period of increasing tensions, the two nations attempted to determine the ownership of the three degrees of territory. Both governments gave proof of ownership dating back to the colonial period and invoked the principle of uti posidetis of 1810. The appeal to colonial documents was no help because the disputed area was one of those unimportant border areas which was not definitely assigned to any administrative subdivision of South America. Neither country would accept the proof of the other, and both were unwilling to compromise. All attempts to reach an accord through diplomatic negotiations failed, and by 1863 the situation was critical. Bolivia severed diplomatic relations with Chile. The Bolivian congress secretly authorized the president to declare war if necessary to maintain the integrity of the national territory or to defend the national honor.

In the following year the Spanish occupation of the Chinchas Islands distracted Chile and Bolivia and led to a temporary agreement. In an attempt to settle a longstanding dispute, Spain sent a commissioner, Sr. Eusebio Salazar y Mazarredo, to Peru to negotiate an agreement in which Spain would recognize the independence of Peru in return for Peru's assumption of the debts remaining from the colonial period. Spain refused to recognize Peruvian independence until Peru assumed her share of the colonial debt, and Peru refused to negotiate until Spain recognized her independence. Both sides refused to compromise. Peru, maintaining she was a nation not a colony, refused to receive Sr. Salazar y Mazarredo as commissioner rather than as envoy entraordinary. Commissioner Salazar y Mazarredo retired from Lima and with the Spanish fleet that had brought him to Peru occupied the Chinchas Islands. He justified his action by stating that Spain had the right to seize the former viceroyalty or any part of it since Spain had not yet recognized the independence of Peru. Public outrage and fear in the Pacific coast nations of South America brought about the convening of the Congress of American Republics in Lima. Chile was represented by one of her most prominent politicians, Manuel Montt, and she allied herself with Peru and Bolivia to jointly defend their independence against Spain.

Although Spain disavowed the seizure of the Chinchas Islands and recalled Salazar, Chileans were not satisfied. The press was violently anti-Spanish, and some acts of disrespect toward the Spanish flag and legation occurred. On September 18, 1865, Admiral José Manuel Pareja, commander of the Spanish squadron, demanded that the Chilean government present a twenty-one gun salute to the Spanish flag as satisfaction for these offenses. If no satisfactory reply were received within four days, relations between the two nations would be terminated. After extending the time limit two days, Admiral Pareja declared relations broken; Chile replied the same day with a declaration of war.

In the early part of the next year Peru, Ecuador, and Bolivia also declared war and joined with Chile in an alliance against Spain.[3] Differences with each other were subordinated in the face of what they considered the Spanish attack on the independence of all the former Pacific coast colonies in South America. Spain had no intention of reconquering her former colonies, nor did she have the resources to do so. Nevertheless, the Pacific states feared Spanish motives, felt threatened, and went to war.

Relations between Chile and Bolivia were resumed with a new attitude of reconciliation on both sides. Negotiations were placed in the hands of the Bolivian minister in Chile, Juan Ramón Muñoz Cabrera, and the

35

Chilean minister of foreign relations, Alvaro Covarrubias. In August of 1866, the two representatives signed a boundary treaty which was ratified and exchanged in December of the same year. [4]

Article one declared the boundary to be the twenty-fourth parallel from the Pacific Ocean to the eastern boundary of Chile. The eastern boundary of Chile was indefinitely stated since Chile and Argentina had not yet agreed upon it. The location of the twenty-fourth parallel was to be determined by a commission of experts, half of whom would be appointed by each nation. This line was to be marked by visible and permanent markers, and the expenses were to be shared equally by both nations.

In article two Chile and Bolivia agreed to divide equally the revenues from guano and mineral deposits located between 23° and 25° latitude. Although a boundary was determined in article one, article two ignored that boundary and substituted a boundary zone in so far as the fiscal administration of one degree of territory belonging to each nation was concerned. Bolivia agreed in article three to pay the cost of constructing port facilities at Mejillones and to open a custom house in that port. Bolivia further agreed to open no other custom house for the exportation of guano or minerals extracted in the shared territory. Under article two Chile would receive half of the revenue from the export tax on guano and minerals collected at the Mejillones custom house. Chile was authorized to name one or more agents to audit the accounts of this custom house to determine her share of the revenues. Bolivia was granted the same rights in any custom houses Chile might establish in her half of the border area. From the beginning this agreement proved unworkable.

In the remaining articles Chile acquired the right to export the products of her territory between 24° and 25° S. through the custom house at Mejillones free of all export duties. Although the term products was not defined, presumably it did not include guano and minerals. No import duties could be imposed on goods for Chile that entered through Mejillones. The system of exploitation or sale of guano as well as the taxes on minerals in the shared zone would be determined jointly by means of a special convention. Neither nation could alienate its rights in the border area to any other state, company, or individual. If one of the contracting parties decided to sell its rights in the area, the buyer could only be the other contracting party. The two nations also agreed to grant the first explorers of the guano deposits at Mejillones an indemnity of eighty thousand pesos, payable with ten percent of the net proceeds from the Mejillones custom house.

Instead of settling the dispute between Chile and Bolivia, the Treaty of 1866 created new problems. Neither government found the treaty satisfactory at the time it was signed, nor did it improve with age. When the fighting with Spain ended in 1866, each nation returned to its former position of resentment and distrust of the other. In this atmosphere the mixed commission began marking the boundary with visible and permanent signs. Using the procedure previously agreed upon, the commission transmitted the boundary line to the foreign office of each country and assumed approval by both when no reply was received from either government. Later the silver mines of Caracoles were discovered within the border zone, just south of the twenty-third parallel as marked by the joint commission. Bolivia stated that the border marked by the commission was not valid until approved by a decree of her government; Chile held that in accordance with the terms of the treaty no approval by either government was necessary. Bolivia proposed a new line that placed the mines of Caracoles solely within Bolivian territory and gave her all the revenue from them. Chile refused to accept the new border.

Article two of the treaty, which provided for equal division of the revenues in the border zone, was a complete failure and a major source of irritation for both nations. Bolivia felt that her sovereignty was infringed by the provisions relating to the custom house at Mejillones. The requirements that she open a custom house at Mejillones and that she export all guano and minerals from the border area through that custom house antagonized her. In spite of the treaty provisions, Bolivia disliked permitting Chilean fiscal agents to audit the accounts of her custom house and resented sharing customs receipts collected at Mejillones.

Bolivia refused to enforce those provisions of the treaty she felt were detrimental to her interests. She exported minerals through Cobija above the twenty-third parallel; her half of the eighty thousand pesos compensating the first explorers of the Mejillones guano deposits was not paid; and she refused to pay Chile half of the customs receipts collected at Mejillones. Chile believed that the only benefits she had derived from the treaty were nullified by Bolivia's selective enforcement. Chile said her concessions, made in the interest of peace, had been made in vain. She felt cheated. On the other hand, Bolivia felt that Chile alone had gained from the treaty. According to Bolivia the treaty had been obtained by sly and underhanded methods from General Mariano Melgarejo, military dictator of Bolivia when the treaty was approved.

In January, 1871, Melgarejo was deposed and a new Bolivian government set up. One of the first decisions of the new government was to annul all of the previous government's acts and international agreements which it chose to consider illegal. The Treaty of 1866 was among those so-called illegal international agreements. Chile refused to recognize the unilateral action of the Bolivian government and declared the treaty still in force. The two nations did agree to negotiate. Bolivia appointed Minister of Foreign Affairs Casimero Corral to represent her, and Chile appointed Santiago Lindsay as her representative.

The Lindsay-Corral Convention, signed in La Paz on December 5, 1872, was essentially a confirmation of the 1866 treaty. [5] The twenty-fourth parallel was retained as the boundary, but the eastern boundary of Chile, previously left vague, was stated as the highest peaks of the Andes. In the event that the boundary-marking commission appointed under the earlier treaty could not reach an agreement on placing boundary markers, a third party chosen by common accord or by the Emperor of Brazil would have the deciding vote. The approval of neither government would be necessary for the boundary marked to be valid. It was hoped that this provision would settle the problem of the mines at Caracoles. The Chilean government accepted the convention within the month following its completion, but the Bolivian congress delayed any discussion of the convention until the congressional session of 1874.

In effect, the postponement was a repudiation of the Lindsay-Corral Convention and necessitated another attempt to reach an accord. Negotiations were immediately resumed and brought to a successful conclusion within a year. A new boundary treaty abrogating and replacing the Treaty of 1866 was signed on August 6, 1874. [6] The twenty-fourth parallel from the Pacific Ocean to the Cordillera of the Andes was retained as the boundary, and the line marked by the commission established by the 1866 treaty was recognized. Any future disagreements over marking the boundary would be settled by two experts, one appointed by each country. In case the experts disagreed the Emperor of Brazil would appoint a third party with the deciding vote. The existing guano and any discovered in the future between 23º and 25º S. would be subject to the halving agreement in effect at the time of the signing of this treaty, and the laws regulating the exportation, administration, and sale of guano already in effect could be changed only by common accord. This clause did not specifically include minerals or the largest source of wealth, nitrates.

In article four Bolivia agreed to maintain the export tax on minerals, including nitrates, at the existing rates. No additional Bolivian taxes could be imposed on the persons, industries, or capital of Chile. It was specifically stated that these provisions were to continue for a period of twenty-five years and were applicable only to the border zone. The fourth article, which later played an extremely important part in the events leading into the War of the Pacific, limited Bolivia's legislative powers in the border zone. After the promulgation of this treaty in October of 1875, Bolivia could not raise the export tax on minerals, nor could she increase the taxes on the nitrate industry in the border zone.

The treaty provided for the free importation of Bolivian and Chilean native products into the littoral between 23º and 25º S. latitude. Bolivia was also required to provide permanent port facilities at Mejillones and Antofagasta. A complementary protocol, signed in June, 1875, and considered an integral part of the treaty, provided for arbitration of all problems arising from the treaty.

The 1874 treaty like its predecessor was a failure. Relations between the two nations did not improve. Bolivia found this treaty no more acceptable than the preceding one. Following much discussion, the Bolivian congress approved the new treaty only after the complementary protocol was signed. Because of her growing mistrust and fear of Chile, Bolivia became more receptive to an alliance with Peru against Chile. Before she signed the new boundary treaty with Chile, Bolivia had signed a secret alliance with Peru. An important consideration leading to the Peruvian-Bolivian Alliance was nitrates. The Peruvian government owned the guano industry in the Chinchas Islands and received a considerable portion of the national revenues from guano. After 1870 Peru found it more and more difficult to meet her financial obligations. War with Spain, government pensions, the foreign debt, and expensive internal improvements raised expenditures above revenues. To increase governmental revenues Peru decided to extend her monopoly over guano to include nitrates. By controlling the two competing products she could increase the income from both and achieve fiscal solvency.

The trouble with this plan was that Peru was not the only source of nitrates and guano. Bolivia possessed extensive deposits of nitrates and lesser deposits of guano in the area in dispute with Chile; therefore, Peru had to obtain Bolivian cooperation in order to control the nitrate and guano supply. The first step in Peru's plan was to offer Bolivia a defensive alliance against Chile. In her struggle with Chile, Bolivia would obtain Peruvian moral support, military aid, and more importantly, naval support. The lack of a navy left Bolivian ports vulnerable to attack by the Chilean navy; a Peruvian alliance would remedy that situation.

The balance of naval power between two Pacific coast nations, Chile and Peru, played an important part in the events leading to the War of the Pacific. Before the outbreak of the war with Spain, Peru had purchased armor-plated steam warships of the smaller class, and she continued to build up her fleet after the war. Peru felt that her national defense required naval superiority over any other Pacific coast nation, especially Chile. Chile assumed that the Peruvian naval preparations were directed against her and reacted by building up her own navy. Beginning in the 1870's Chile purchased modern warships to match those of Peru. A minor naval race developed. Until 1876 the warships that each nation had ordered in Europe were not yet completed, and both sides avoided open conflict. The outbreak of war would have resulted in internment of the new warships not yet delivered.

Bolivia, though not involved in the naval race, was vitally concerned with its progress. The geography of Bolivia made it impossible to defend her ports without a navy. Communications between the coast and the center of the republic were limited; there was no railroad nor telegraph line from the coast to the interior. The intervening desert made troop movement on a large scale almost impossible and presented a supply problem of the greatest magnitude. As Chile was to learn later, an army had to carry in addition to regular military supplies every need of both men and animals, including water and fodder. No supplies were available in the desert. Bolivia experienced these same supply problems in defending the area or transporting troops from the central plateau to the coast.

Both Bolivia and Peru saw an advantage in an alliance. They signed a secret treaty creating a defensive alliance in February, 1873. [7] The signatory nations mutually guaranteed the independence and integrity of their respective territories from the aggression of any country or any filibustering force without a national allegiance. The alliance could be offensive if another state attempted to infringe the sovereignty of any portion of the national territory of either contracting party. Both nations reserved the right to decide in each case if the conditions in the treaty were fulfilled and when mutual assistance would go into effect. The assistance included severing diplomatic relations with the aggressor nation, closing ports to the offending nation, and prohibiting imports.

The treaty provided for naming delegates to draw up a protocol of cooperation in the event the treaty were violated by a third nation. The protocol would determine the subsidies and the land, naval, and auxiliary forces that each country would be required to furnish for the defense of the alliance. Cooperation between the naval and military forces and joint planning were also agreed to. It was specifically stated that each country assumed the obligations outlined in the proposed protocol even if no protocol were signed. The terms of the treaty did not extend to any civil strife within either country.

Neither nation could conclude a peace, truce, or armistice without the concurrence of the other, nor could either concede to any nation territory or privileges which would reduce or limit its independence or sovereignty. The two republics agreed not to negotiate boundary treaties with-

out each other's knowledge. They pledged to exhaust all means of concil-
iation, including arbitration by a third power, to prevent a rupture or to
end a war if one had already started.

Peru with the alliance protected her interest in nitrates and guano.
Bolivia could not cede to Chile nitrate areas, conclude a boundary treaty
unfavorable to Peru, or grant to Chile mineral rights that would threaten
Peruvian interests. At the same time Peru felt that she had placed herself in a position to offer armed mediation between Chile and Bolivia, but
her position was not as strong as she hoped. Her attempt to mediate the
dispute in 1879, when war between Chile and Bolivia seemed imminent,
was unsuccessful.

Article ten of the treaty provided for separate or joint attempts to
expand the defensive alliance to include another or other American nations.
The other American nation that might have been persuaded to join the secret alliance against Chile was Argentina, who was also involved in a boundary dispute with Chile. Although Peru and Bolivia urged her to join, Argentina refused. The Argentine congress secretly debated the treaty; the
lower house approved, but the matter was dropped when the senate disap-
proved. Argentina did not want to get involved in the politics of the Pacific
states, nor did she want to fight Peru's war with Chile. She was sure that
entering the alliance would result in both.

Another reason Argentina rejected the proposed alliance was her
boundary dispute with Bolivia. The Argentine government decided that the
boundary question should be settled before any alliance was signed. The
Argentine refusal meant that Peru did not accomplish her objective of al-
lying the surrounding nations against Chile. Chile feared that Peru would
make such an effort and felt the danger of its succeeding was very real
since she had boundary disputes with Bolivia and Argentina.

An additional article attached at the end of the Treaty of 1873 provided that the treaty would remain secret until by common accord the two
nations deemed publication necessary. However, rumors of a secret treaty
circulated through the diplomatic corps in Peru and Argentina almost as
soon as the treaty was signed, long before the existence of the secret treaty
was definitely established. Chile and Brazil each had reason to believe that
Peru was directing the alliance against her. So when rumors of a secret
treaty began to circulate, the question was not whether such a treaty existed
but against whom the alliance was aimed. Chile and Brazil, each fearing
for herself, worked together to get information.

Historians disagree on how successful Chile was in obtaining information about the Peruvian-Bolivian Alliance. Peruvian and Bolivian writers agree that Chile did know about the treaty. They emphasize the fact

41

that the treaty passed through three diplomatic corps and was placed before the legislatures of three countries. With that many opportunities for leaks no treaty could remain absolutely secret. These writers say that since the alliance was only defensive, it was not a threat to Chile.

Most Chilean historians maintain that the secret treaty was directed against Chile and posed a threat to her sovereignty; the fact that the treaty was secret proved that it contained sinister plans. These writers state that the Chilean government had heard rumors of the secret treaty but it did not see a copy until 1879. Although Chilean officials strongly suspected the existence of a treaty, they could take no official action. The secrecy made Chile fear the treaty even more. Chilean writers say that all Chile's fears were well-founded, for the publication of the treaty proved Chile's suspicions to be true.

One effect of the Peruvian-Bolivian Alliance was to make Bolivia less willing to compromise her differences with Chile. Bolivia felt greatly strengthened by her military alliance with Peru, who was reputed to be the strongest nation on the Pacific coast of South America. She, therefore, not only refused to compromise but also repudiated the Treaty of 1866. Bolivia demanded that Chile change the 1866 treaty to incorporate Bolivian interests. Because she was not prepared to resist these demands at that time, Chile accepted modifications in favor of Bolivia and signed a new treaty in 1874. By 1875 conditions had changed; Argentina had refused to join the Peruvian-Bolivian Alliance, and Chile had increased her naval strength to approximately that of Peru. Chile, then, became less willing to compromise. Under these circumstances war became probable.

The incident which precipitated the war involved article four of the treaty of 1874. This article reads:

> The export duties which are imposed on minerals exploited in the zone of which the preceding articles speak will not exceed the quota which is at present collected and Chilean persons, industries, and capital will not be subject to more contributions of any class whatso-ever than those which exist at the present. The stipulation contained in this article will last for the term of twenty-five years. [8]

The Antofagasta Railroad and Nitrate Company, a Chilean company, had acquired through purchase and contracts with the Bolivian government a large nitrate concession. The company operated near Antofagasta in the border zone and, consequently, was protected by article four of the Treaty of 1874. Furthermore, the company had been granted additional concessions in a contract with the Bolivian government. This contract predated the Treaty of 1874. When Mariano Melgarejo was overthrown in 1871, the Bolivian congress annulled all nitrate concessions granted by Melgarejo on the grounds that they were illegal. In order to obtain funds Melgarejo, offering very liberal terms, had sold the right to develop Bolivian minerals and nitrate deposits to foreigners. These sales included nitrate concessions to Chileans. To replace its annulled concession the Antofagasta Railroad and Nitrate Company obtained another grant, this one dated November 27, 1873. [9] The new concession, located near Antofagasta, was smaller in size and had specifically stated limits in contrast to the old concession which was not only larger but also located only generally in the desert of Atacama. The new concession was granted for fifteen years, starting January 1, 1874, and included the right to export nitrates through the port of Antofagasta free of all export duties and any other regulations including municipal laws.

After General Hilarión Daza came to power by military coup in May, 1878, these guarantees were not honored by his government. Three months before Daza's accession to power, the Bolivian legislature, seeking additional revenues, had passed a law approving the 1873 contract on condition that the Antofagasta Company pay a minimum of ten centavos per quintal of nitrates exported. [10] Bolivia found this tax eminently satisfactory because her nationals would not pay it and because Peru would support it. Peru's interest in controlling nitrate prices assured her support of a tax on Chilean nitrates. Although the tax was not considered exorbitant, both the Chilean government and the Antofagasta Company considered the tax illegal because it violated article four of the Treaty of 1874 and clause four of the contract of 1873.

In April, 1871, execution of the law was indefinitely suspended as a result of an agreement reached by the Chilean minister in La Paz, Pedro Nolasco Videla, and the Bolivian minister of finance, Manuel J. Salvatierra. [11] When General Daza assumed the presidential powers, negotiations were in progress to achieve a permanent solution acceptable to both countries. But despite sustained discussions, no permanent solution could be reached. In December President Daza instructed the minister of finance to order compliance with the law. [12] This order, dated December 17, instructed lower officials to collect the export tax imposed upon the Antofagasta Company from the date of the promulgation of the law, a period of ten months. The Antofagasta Company continued to refuse to pay the new export tax. On January 11, 1879, the prefect of Cobija, the official in charge of the area in which the company operated, ordered the arrest of George Hicks, the manager of the Antofagasta Company, for failure to pay the export tax. At the same time the prefect also ordered the seizure of company property in a sufficient amount to cover the debt, considered by Bolivia to amount to 90,948 bolivianos and 13 centavos.[13] Mr. Hicks fled to the Chilean warship Blanco Encalada anchored in the harbor of Antofagasta, where he was granted asylum.[14] On January 14 the captain of the port of Antofagasta, Exequiel Apodaca, prohibited the loading of nitrate for export by the Company.[15] The Company was forced to suspend operations, causing immediate unemployment for more than two thousand workers, most of whom were Chilean.[16] The economic life of Antofagasta was dependent upon the nitrate works, and business activity almost ceased when the Company shut down. On February 1 the Bolivian government declared the 1873 contract with the Antofagasta Company rescinded.[17] The nitrate concession which had been granted to the Company reverted to the state. The Antofagasta Company was ruined; its property was confiscated to pay the export tax, and its nitrate concessions were annulled. The plight of the Antofagasta Company was of great concern to the Chilean government.

Negotiations between the two nations had been proceeding for almost a year. It was not until the temporary suspension of the new export tax was ended unilaterally by Bolivia that trouble developed. Both nations accepted the principle of arbitration which had been included in the Treaty of 1874 to settle any differences arising from the meaning or execution of the treaty. So the next step toward a solution to their difficulties should have been arbitration, but by December, 1878, when Bolivia ordered enforcement of the new nitrate tax law, no arbitration agreement had been reached. After December arbitration was impossible. Chile declared that a necessary condition for arbitration was suspension of the tax law.[18] Bolivia replied that she could not negotiate peacefully with the Chilean warship Blanco Encalada anchored at Antofagasta.

On February 5 the Antofagasta Company received notice that the company property seized by the Bolivian government would be sold at auction for payment of the export tax. The following day the Bolivian foreign minister officially notified Chile that the Antofagasta Company's nitrate contract had been rescinded and that as a result of the revocation the execution of the nitrate tax law of February, 1878, would be suspended. The Bolivian foreign minister added that since the cause of the Chilean protest was no longer in force there was no need for a direct settlement or for arbitration. Harmonious relations and good understanding between the two nations could now be restored. However, the nitrate concession was still canceled, and the Company was ruined. Chile did not feel that this was a satisfactory solution to the problem.

The Chilean minister, on February 8, sent a forty-eight hour ultimatum requesting the arbitration to which Bolivia earlier had agreed in principle. After an interval of four days with no reply, he closed the Chilean legation and requested his passport. He declared the Treaty of 1874 broken by Bolivia's failure to comply with the obligations imposed upon her by that agreement. In the absence of a valid treaty, Chile reasserted her rights to the littoral claimed before the Treaty of 1866 and served notice that she would take any action necessary to protect her rights. One of these actions was to send an expeditionary force to occupy Antofagasta. The Chilean force assumed control of the city on February 4, the date set for the sale of all the property of the Antofagasta Company. The Chilean commander, Colonel Emilio Sotomayor, ordered the property in dispute returned to the company, which resumed operations after a short period of time.

The day the Chilean troops occupied Antofagasta was the first day of a ten-day celebration of the birthday of President Daza. Although the news of the Chilean military action was known to Daza, it was not released to the public until the end of the celebration. On March 1 Bolivia declared war on Chile and gave Chilean citizens ten days to leave the country.[19] All Chilean owned property was confiscated.

In spite of the Bolivian declaration of war, Peru sent a special envoy, José Antonio Lavalle, to Chile to negotiate an arbitration agreement between Chile and Bolivia.[20] Peru proposed, as an essential condition for arbitration, the withdrawal of Chilean troops from the disputed area. Because Chile could not protect the Antofagasta Company if she withdrew, she refused to accept this condition. Chile also questioned the sincerity of the Peruvian efforts. While these negotiations were taking place Chile learned of military preparations in Peru from Joaquin Godoi, her minister in Lima. Minister Godoi reported troop movements into the southern provinces and a trip to Europe by Vice-President José Francisco Canevaro to purchase war supplies and one or more warships. Chile suspected that the arbitration negotiation was only a device to gain time so Peru could obtain war materiel before neutral countries embargoed them.

Another complicating factor was the rumor circulating in Chile of an alliance between Bolivia and Peru. When asked about it, Sr. Lavalle replied that he had no knowledge of any alliance. He further stated that while he was president of the diplomatic commission of congress in 1874, 1876, and 1878 no treaty was approved. The Chilean government found this answer unsatisfactory and instructed Minister Godoi in Lima to ask for a declaration of neutrality from Peru. On the night of March 20 President Mariano I. Prado talked privately with the Chilean minister. When pressed for a declaration of neutrality, President Prado said that Peru could not declare neutrality because she had a defensive and offensive alliance with Bolivia. Chile immediately terminated the arbitration discussions and severed diplomatic relations with Peru. On April 5, 1879, Chile declared war on Bolivia and Peru, and the War of the Pacific officially began.

The next day President Prado informed his countrymen of the Bolivian alliance and recognized the casus foederis. In effect Peru was declaring war on Chile because under the terms of the alliance Peru was required to give Bolivia aid as soon as the casus foederis was declared.

Even before the declaration of war Chile had expanded into some of the disputed territory. Following the occupation of Antofagasta, Chile claimed the territory south of the twenty-third parallel as a result of Bolivia's nullification of the boundary treaty of 1874. She immediately occupied this area, and as soon as war was declared she occupied the few remaining centers of population in the Bolivian littoral. After Chile moved into the littoral, Bolivia's only access to outside supplies was through Peru.

The War of the Pacific can be divided into two parts, naval battles and land campaigns. Since Bolivia had no navy, only Chile and Peru participated in the struggle for supremacy of the seas. This was an important phase of the war, for the ocean was the only practical means of transportation north and south. There were no north and south railroad lines; in both Chile and Peru the railroads ran from the coast eastward to inland cities. Bolivia had no railroads or telegraph lines from the coast to the interior cities on the altiplano. Control of the sea was necessary for a successful defensive or offensive campaign.

When war broke out the Chilean navy had recently acquired two modern armor-plated warships to strengthen the existing fleet of six smaller wooden ships. The Peruvian navy comprised six ships, four of which were ironclad. Two of the Peruvian ships, the Manco Capac and the Atahualpa, were floating fortresses, not seagoing vessels. The first was stationed at Arica and the second at Callao.

On April 5, 1879, the day Chile declared war, the Chilean navy under the command of Juan Williams Rebolledo, the son of the commander of the 1842 expedition to the Strait of Magellan, established the blockade of Iquique. The plan of Admiral Williams was to force the Peruvian navy into action by blockading and raiding neighboring ports. For about six weeks the Chilean navy continued the blockade of Iquique but did not move against Arica, the other Peruvian port in the South. Peru sent troops and supplies into Arica. The Chilean government, backed by public opinion, compelled Admiral Williams to change his strategy; so Admiral Williams decided to attack Callao, the main port of Peru. In the middle of May most of the Chilean navy sailed north for Callao. The Esmeralda and the Covadonga, slow wooden ships unfit for an extended sea voyage, remained at Iquique to continue the blockade.

On the same day the Chilean squadron sailed north, a Peruvian fleet left Callao for Arica, transporting troops and supplies and carrying President Prado south to assume command of the Allied Army. The two fleets passed each other at sea without realizing it. When President Prado arrived in Arica, he was informed that the blockade of Iquique had been weakened. He ordered the two Peruvian ironclads, the Huascar and the Independencia, to capture the two Chilean ships and break the blockade. The Peruvian ships arrived at Iquique on May 21; the Huascar engaged the Esmeralda and the Independencia, the Covadonga.[12] The Peruvian ironclads were superior to the Chilean wooden ships in every way, including speed, size, and strength. During a four-hour battle the Huascar three times rammed the Esmeralda, which sank with her colors still flying. On the first ramming Captain Arturo Pratt of the Esmeralda led a boarding party onto the deck of the Huascar. Only Captain Pratt had jumped aboard when the ships parted, leaving him on the deck of the Huascar alone. He died fighting and became a national hero, bolstering the morale of Chile.

The Covadonga was hit early in the battle and began taking water. She fled southward with the Independencia in pursuit. About ten miles south of Iquique the Covadonga crossed a rocky shoal off Point Grueso. The Independencia, which drew more water, struck the shoal with such force that her bow was lifted out of the water and the keel was broken. In this position her guns could not be trained on the Chilean ship that turned back and circled her, blowing holes below the waterline. The crew abandoned ship and was rescued by the Huascar, which had followed after sinking her opponent. Meanwhile, the Covadonga escaped southward. Peru claimed a victory because she had sunk one Chilean ship and broken the blockade. Chile achieved a greater victory by sinking one of Peru's two ironclads. Naval supremacy depended upon ironclads and steel ships.

The Huascar returned the survivors to Callao and then cruised the waters off Chile harassing Chilean shipping and bombarding unprotected port cities. Accompanied by the Union, she was able to elude the entire Chilean navy, which sought her for more than four months. On October 8, while returning to Peru to obtain coal and supplies, she encountered an enemy squadron. The speedy Union escaped out to sea, but the Huascar was slower and could not keep up. The Huascar attempted to flee northward and encountered another Chilean squadron coming from that direction. In the ensuing Battle of Angamos, the Huascar was forced to fight both Chilean squadrons alone. Several shells penetrated her armor destroying the wheel, rudder, and communications system and killing Admiral Miguel Grau, who was in command, and all three of her other senior officers. Her

47

steering mechanism destroyed, the Huascar circled to the right while the Chilean ironclads Blanco Encalada and Almirante Cochrane fired into her. After an hour the Huascar surrendered, and a Chilean crew boarded her to tow her to port. Although the Union escaped, the Peruvian navy was so reduced in power by the loss of the ironclads that Chile gained supremacy on the sea.

Naval supremacy enabled Chile to transport troops and supplies to any point along the coast of Bolivia or Peru. Chilean strategy was based upon this supremacy and the lack of overland transportation north and south in all three countries. Chile planned to hop north from one port to the next, occupying the Bolivian littoral and the southern provinces of Peru. Chile expected to force the capitulation of her enemies through the loss of national territory and the loss of revenue from the minerals in the area. This plan began with the invasion of the southernmost Peruvian province, Tarapacá, in October, 1879. The campaign of Tarapacá lasted about a month and resulted in the retreat of the Allied Armies, leaving Chile in complete control of the disputed territory that had caused difficulties before the war. Before the declaration of war Chile had occupied the Bolivian province of Antafagasta.

The loss of the southern provinces caused revolutions in both Peru and Bolivia. President Prado of Peru returned to Lima where he remained until the middle of December. Unexpectedly and without explanation he sailed to Europe. The vice-president assumed his office but was able to retain it less than a week. Nicolás de Piérola, a prominent politician and military leader, established himself as Supreme Chief of the Republic. Shortly after the Peruvian revolution, General Daza was deposed by his own troops, and General Eleodoro Camacho became commander of the Bolivian army. A revolution in La Paz at the same time gave General Narciso Campero political leadership of the nation. About six months later, in June, 1880, General Campero was elected president of Bolivia.

Since her victories did not produce the expected surrender, Chile decided to extend her conquest farther north into the adjoining Peruvian departments of Tacna and Moquegua. Chile planned to make a landing on the coast of Moquegua and cut off the southern provinces from supplies and reinforcements. The landing was successfully accomplished during the last part of February and the first week of March, 1880. The march inland culminated in the Battle of Los Angeles on March 22. The Chilean victory in that battle isolated the Peruvian army in the southern provinces and permitted Chile by June to obtain control of the remaining territory in Tacna and Arica. The Moquegua campaign ended with Chile in control of Peru from the department of Moquegua south through Tacna, Arica, and Tara-

48

paca. Chile also held the Bolivian coastal province of Antofagasta and,
for all practical purposes, had eliminated Bolivia from the war.

Despite her losses Peru still did not surrender. Chile, therefore,
deemed it necessary to occupy Lima and Callao in order to end the war.
Preparations delayed the beginning of the next campaign for four months.
In mid November a Chilean army numbering 25,000 made landings at Pisco,
about one hundred twenty-five miles south of Lima, and at Curayaco, twenty-
five miles farther south. Not until January, 1881, were preparations and
organization completed for the march upon Lima. During the interval Peru
hastily organized defenses for Lima. The first line of defense was located
about ten miles from Lima and extended six miles inland from Los Chorri-
llos. The defense of Lima was entrusted to an army of civilians hastily
recruited, ill-trained, and poorly armed. The untrained army of Peru
was unable to stop the Chilean army when it advanced on the first line of
defense on January 13 and was forced to fall back on the second line of defense at Miraflores on the outskirts of Lima. A truce, arranged by the
diplomatic corps in Lima in an attempt to avoid damage to the city, was
unintentionally broken on January 15 when General Manuel Baquedano, commander in chief of the Chilean army, was fired upon while inspecting his
front lines. The action became general and resulted in the Battle of Miraflores. Before the end of the day, the Peruvian battle line broke, leaving
the capital defenseless. Two days later the Chilean army occupied Lima,
ending formal resistance by Peru.

NOTES

1. Anguita, Leyes, pp. 392-393.
2. For a good, brief collection of documents concerning the outbreak of
    war, the peace treaty, and arbitration of Tacna-Arica see William
    Jefferson Dennis, Documentary History of the Tacna-Arica Dispute,
    University of Iowa Studies in the Social Sciences, 8, no. 3 (Iowa
    City, 1927).
3. For terms of the alliance see Aurelio Bascuñan Montes, Recopilación
    de tratados y convenciones celebrados entre la República de Chile
    y las Potencias Extranjeras, 7 vols. (Santiago: Imprenta Cervan-
    tes, 1894-1916), 2, pp. 4-16.
4. The treaty is printed in Bascuñan Montes, Recopilación, 2, pp. 22-28.

5. See República de Chile, Oficina de Mensura de Tierras, La Línea de Frontera con la República de Bolivia (Santiago: Sociedad Imprenta y Litografía Universo, 1910), pp. 19-20.

6. For the treaty and complementary protocol see Bascuñan Montes, Recopiliación, 2, pp. 101-107.

7. República de Peru, Ministerio de Relaciones Exteriores, Colección de los Tratados, Convenciones, Capitulaciones, Armisticios y otros actos diplomáticos y politicos celebrados desde la Independencia hasta el dia, precidida de una introdución que comprende la época colonial, 14 vols. (Lima: Imprenta del Estado, 1890-1911), 2, pp. 440-444.

8. Bascuñan Montes, Recopilación, 2, p. 130.

9. Pascual Ahumada Moreno, Guerra del Pacifico Recopilación completa de todo los documentos officiales, correspondencias, y demas publicaciones referentes a la guerra que ha dado a luz la prensa de Chile, Peru y Bolivia, conteniendo documentos inéditos de importancia, 3 vols. (Valparaiso: Imprenta del Progreso, 1884-1891), 1, pp. 9-11.

10. Ahumada Moreno, Guerra del Pacifico, 1, p. 11.

11. Ahumada Moreno, Guerra del Pacifico, 1, pp. 15-16. Note from Chilean Minister in Bolivia to Bolivian Minister of Foreign Affairs, dated La Paz, July 2, 1878.

12. Ahumada Moreno, Guerra del Pacifico, 1, p. 22.

13. Ahumada Moreno, Guerra del Pacifico, 1, p. 23.

14. Ahumada Moreno, Guerra del Pacifico, 1, p. 23. Note from Chilean Consul General in Antofagasta to Chilean Minister of Foreign Affairs, dated Antofagasta, January 12, 1879.

15. Ahumada Moreno, Guerra del Pacifico, 1, p. 26.

16. Ahumada Moreno, Guerra del Pacifico, 1, pp. 30-31. Note from Chilean Consul General in Antofagasta to Chilean Minister of Foreign Affairs, dated Antofagasta, February 7, 1879.

17. Ahumada Moreno, Guerra del Pacifico, 1, p. 26.

18. The official communications and notes of the Bolivian and Chilean Ministers are printed in Ahumada Moreno, Guerra del Pacifico, 1.

19. Ahumada Moreno, Guerra del Pacifico, 1, pp. 101-102.

20. The official communications are printed in Ahumada Moreno, Guerra del Pacifico, 1.

21. Reports of the Chilean naval commanders are printed in Ahumada Moreno, Guerra del Pacifico, 1.

CHAPTER 4. THE PEACE TREATIES

AFTER the fall of Lima no organized resistance could be offered
by Peru, and, for all practical purposes, the War of the Pacific was over.
Chile occupied the heavily populated and highly productive area which included the two major cities of Lima and Callao. President Nicolás de Pi-
erola fled into the interior and attempted to continue the war. He soon
realized that further resistance was detrimental to the best interest of his
country and proposed peace negotiations. Chile refused to deal with his
government unless he retracted a letter in which he blamed Chile for
breaking the truce before the Battle of Miraflores. Although President
Piérola eventually complied, Chile continued to refuse to recognize his
government. Chile faced the problem of finding or establishing a government that would cooperate with her by negotiating a peace satisfactory to
Chile.

Foreign intervention was prevented by the attitude of the United
States. The North American government refused to join European nations
in mediation. It was the position of the United States that such action
could be called coercion. European countries realized that they could not
take action on their own without the cooperation or consent of the United
States.

The United States had made one attempt at mediation in late October, 1880. This effort ended in complete failure. The failure can be
partially attributed to a misunderstanding among the United States ministers in Chile, Peru, and Bolivia about the objectives and the procedures
of the conference. Actually, little real interest was shown by the United
States government. Instructions from Washington were rather meager,
and those that were sent were vague. No one in Washington offered effective over-all guidance, and the three men in the Latin American capitals tended to be sympathetic with the point of view of the country in which
each resided.

Mr. Thomas Osborn, United States minister in Chile and senior
minister at the conference, ensured the failure of the meeting by stating

that the United States would not take an active part in the discussions. The Latin American states involved in the war entered the conference with a complete lack of enthusiasm. Peru was displeased because Chile continued the Peruvian campaign while the conference was in session. Bolivia was confident that the discussions would end in failure because Chile insisted upon the cession of Tarapacá, which Peru would not cede. The Chilean government was reluctant to become associated with any peace effort for domestic reasons. In Chile, victories had created enthusiasm for the war and a popular demand for the capture of Lima. In spite of a general feeling among the principals that the conference was predisposed to failure, a meeting was arranged aboard the U. S. Lackawana, anchored in the Bay of Arica.

Since no pressure would be exerted by the United States, Chile felt free to present terms which were in effect a declaration of Chilean victory. Her terms included an indemnity and the cession of the Peruvian and Bolivian provinces of Tacna, Arica, Tarapacá, and Antofagasta. Not only would such an acquisition of territory give Chile all of the nitrate resources of her two northern neighbors, it would also give her all of the Bolivian coastline. Neither Bolivia nor Peru found these terms acceptable; Chile refused to accept anything less. Mr. Osborn continued to limit the role of the United States. The conference ended in failure, and the delegates returned to their own countries with peace no closer. Chile then decided to end the war by military means rather than by negotiations and in November began the last campaign, the invasion of Peru and the capture of Lima.

After the collapse of Peru, Chile was in no hurry to sign a peace treaty. In fact, she found the war quite profitable. Considerable amounts of property were confiscated and sent to Chile. The expenses of the occupying army were paid by levying war contributions upon the occupied areas. A decree issued in March, 1881, imposed a contribution of one million pesos a month upon a specified list of wealthy men in Lima and Callao. [1] Shortly thereafter, a group of these citizens met and elected Francisco García Calderón, a young Lima lawyer, provisional president. The new government, located in unoccupied Magdalena near Lima, existed with the aid and approval of the Chilean occupational forces. President García Calderón issued a call for a legislature. At this point the United States recognized the new Peruvian government. Encouraged by his initial success, President García Calderón refused to accept the cession of Tarapacá as a condition for peace.

García Calderón's display of resistance to Chilean demands gained him considerable support even among the followers of Piérola. His recognition by the Chilean army had made many fear that García Calderón

52

was a tool of Chile; their fears were now dispelled. Additional popular support made it possible for the new president to organize a stable government for the entire country. These developments caused other foreign powers to begin to recognize the Garcia Calderón government. The Chilean authorities would not permit the Garcia Calderón government to thwart their peace plans; in September, 1881, Chile ordered the arrest and deportation of Garcia Calderón and the termination of his government. The Peruvian government had anticipated such an eventuality and had provided for continuation of the government by electing Admiral Lizardo Montero vice-president and granting him authority to exercise executive power if Garcia Calderón were unable to do so. Admiral Montero's position in the South at Arequipa was not under Chilean control.

Meanwhile, General Andrés Cáceres, who had been appointed by President Piérola to administer the interior departments of Peru, was proclaimed Supreme Head of State by his army. President Piérola's position had become untenable: the Chilean occupational authorities had repudiated his government; the United States had recognized a rival government; and his subordinates were deserting him. He resigned, and after one last attempt to obtain peace without the cession of territory, he left the country. In 1881 political conditions in Peru were in a state of confusion and satisfactory to no one. President Piérola had resigned and was in exile; Provisional President Garcia Calderón was a prisoner in Chile; Vice-President Montero received support from the occupied area and the South; General Cáceres ruled the interior; and General Miguel Iglesias exercised local control in the North. Another national government appeared in August of 1882 when General Iglesias, who favored peace with Chile even if the cession of national territory were necessary, proclaimed himself president.

The Chilean government realized that the occupation of Peru could not continue indefinitely and hoped to be able to conclude peace on its own terms with the Iglesias government. This hope seemed well-founded when President Iglesias convened an assembly at Cajamarca in December, 1882. The assembly called for an immediate peace that did not threaten national independence nor retard national progress. [2] Peace could be concluded in accord with Bolivia or separately. The statement of the Cajamarca assembly was interpreted by Iglesias as authorization to negotiate peace on the basis of the surrender of Tarapacá. Chile responded promptly by presenting to President Iglesias proposed terms which included the unconditional surrender of Tarapacá, the sale of Tacna and Arica to Chile for ten million pesos, a declaration that the territory ceded or sold would not carry a debt, a commercial agreement, and an indemnity for losses suffered by

Chilean citizens in Peru during the war. A preliminary agreement, differing only slightly from the original terms, was drawn up by representatives of Chile and Iglesias during March, April, and May. Before Chile would formally recognize the government of Iglesias, he had to sign this preliminary agreement.

The preliminary agreement contained a promise by Iglesias to sign a peace treaty as soon as his government was recognized by Chile. It was further stipulated that the peace treaty Iglesias promised to sign would include the seven conditions in the preliminary agreement. The first condition was the perpetual and unconditional cession of Tarapacá. Subsequent conditions dealt with the surrender of Tacna and Arica, the Chilean contract for the sale of a million tons of guano from Peru, and other commercial relations. Tacna and Arica were to be subject to Chilean law and authority for ten years after which a plebiscite would determine to which country the provinces would ultimately belong. The country obtaining sovereignty would pay the other nation ten million pesos. Under the terms of the proposed treaty Peru would recognize the validity of the guano contract granted by Chile during the occupation and permit Chile to continue to control the Lobos Islands until the guano contract was fulfilled. The Lobos Islands, also known as the Guano Islands, were the main source of guano for fulfilling the contract. Peru, however, was to receive fifty percent of the guano receipts upon ratification of the peace treaty. A provision for a later agreement on questions of commercial relations, indemnity, and debts owed to Chilean citizens would complete the peace treaty. Chile recognized the government of General Manuel Iglesias on October 18, 1883, and on October 23 the Treaty of Ancón was signed by the new government. The same day the treaty was signed, Chilean occupational forces withdrew from Lima and Callao and President Iglesias entered the capital.

The Treaty of Ancón contained fourteen articles, nine of which were concerned with guano or nitrates. This fact was later cited as proof that Chile's motive for fighting the War of the Pacific was profits from guano and nitrates. Specific terms in the treaty that are used as proof of this charge by Chile's accusers include the cession of the nitrate province of Tarapacá, Chilean administration for ten years of the provinces of Tacna and Arica, continued occupation by Chile of the Guano Islands, and the requirement that Peru conclude an accord with Chile for the exploitation of any nitrates which might be discovered in Peruvian territory.

Most of the treaty was executed without difficulty even though it was unpopular in Peru. The arbitration to settle war debts owed to Chileans, legalizing the acts of the Chilean occupational forces, and even the cession of Tarapacá caused little trouble. However, article three, which provided for Chilean occupation of Tacna and Arica for ten years after which a plebiscite would determine ownership, caused a controversy of long standing.

Article three defines the boundaries of Tacna and Arica. On the north the boundary is described as the River Sama from its source in the cordillera on the frontier of Bolivia to its mouth at the sea; on the south as the ravine and River Camarones; on the west, the Pacific Ocean; and on the east, the Republic of Bolivia. The article also states that Tacna and Arica shall be subject to Chilean law and authority for a period of ten years to be reckoned from the date of the ratification of the treaty of peace. At the expiration of the ten year period a plebiscite will decide by popular vote which nation will receive the territory. The nation that receives the area will pay to the other ten million pesos in Chilean silver or Peruvian soles of equal weight and fineness. The final paragraph of the article provides for a special protocol, to be considered an integral part of the treaty, to prescribe the manner in which the plebiscite would be carried out and the terms for payment of the ten million pesos.

A complementary protocol signed on the same day as the treaty provided for the continued occupation of Peru until the treaty was ratified, enumerated rights for the army of occupation, and authorized Chile to occupy any area of Peru deemed necessary by the Chilean commander-in-chief. Chile did not occupy Lima or Callao but did remain in other portions of Peru until ratification of the Treaty of Ancón was exchanged on March 28, 1884. The plebiscite in Tacna and Arica was supposed to be held ten years from that date.

At the same time that peace negotiations were being held between Chile and the Iglesias government, Chile was conducting a military campaign against Arequipa, the stronghold of Admiral Montero. Since Bolivia had not yet consented to peace discussions, Chile considered extending this campaign into Bolivia. Faced by the threat of an invasion, Bolivia accepted the idea of a truce and authorized E. de Ojeda to propose an armistice to the Chilean government. Ojeda, recently appointed Spanish minister in Uruguay, had not yet left his former position as first secretary of the Spanish legation in Lima. In October, 1883, Ojeda requested a meeting with the Chilean minister of foreign affairs, Luis Aldunate, to discuss Bolivian peace proposals. Aldunate, who was in Lima, notified President Domingo Santa María of the Bolivian proposal. President Santa María was anxious to conclude peace settlements with Peru and Bolivia and sent a French citizen, Gabriel Larrieu, to La Paz as the official representative of Chile. Larrieu persuaded Bolivia to name Belisario Salinas and Belisario Boeta delegates to discuss peace proposals in Valparaiso.

During the first meeting, held on December 7, the Bolivian delegates proposed that Tacna and Arica be transferred to Bolivia. Such a transfer would not only give Bolivia a seaport to replace the littoral she had lost to Chile but would also solve the problem of those provinces without the necessity of holding a plebiscite. Aldunate refused to consider the proposal because Chile, under the Treaty of Ancón, did not have sovereignty over Tacna and Arica. Chile could not dispose of territory which she did not possess. Instead, Aldunate proposed an indefinite truce to provide time for further discussions.

The transfer of Tacna and Arica to Bolivia was not a new idea. Chile had made the same proposal to Bolivia before the war and again during the first stage of the war. The earlier proposals were conditioned upon the transfer of the Bolivian province of Antofagasta to Chile. Bolivia had rejected the earlier proposal because of her reluctance to relinquish Antofagasta to Chile and because of the Peruvian alliance. Now Chile refused to accept the transfer in spite of the fact that she had approved it earlier. One reason for the Chilean attitude was the fact that she occupied Antofagasta and no longer needed to trade any territory for it. Chile also feared that Peru approved of the transfer in order to put Tacna and Arica in the hands of a weak nation from whom Peru could later easily recover them. Moreover, Chile maintained that Bolivia had had her chance to obtain a seaport and had refused it; after losing the war Bolivia should not gain from the peace treaty the great advantage Tacna and Arica represented. The "question of the Pacific," as Bolivia's lack of a seaport is called, has been a factor in Bolivian politics since the War of the Pacific.

When the Bolivian delegates discovered that Chile would not consent to Bolivian ownership of Tacna and Arica, they refused to accept an immediate truce. Chile insisted upon a truce in order to delay peace negotiations until after the plebiscite, which Chile was confident would give her Tacna and Arica. Chile could then exchange the two provinces for the permanent acquisition of Antofagasta. Bolivia lost interest in further negotiations and began to make preparations to resist a Chilean invasion. Resumption of the war seemed imminent in March, 1884, when a last attempt to maintain peace was successful.

An indefinite truce was signed on April 4, 1884. [4] Because of the problems involved in drawing up a peace treaty, no attempt to do so was made. Both nations did pledge to continue negotiations for peace. The Pact of Truce, as the agreement was called, provided for the return of the property of Chilean citizens confiscated by Bolivia during the war and for the re-establishment of commercial relations. The two nations agreed to set up a commission to arbitrate the damage claims of Chilean citizens.

56

Acts by subordinate officials in either country which changed the conditions established by the truce would not be allowed.

The truce also provided for Bolivian use of a seaport in northern Chile. The port of Arica became the port of entry for Bolivia. Chile was authorized to collect the duties on goods imported by Bolivia. Twenty-five percent of the proceeds of the Arica custom house would be paid to Chile for the expenses of the custom house and for goods used in Arica. The remaining seventy-five percent belonged to Bolivia, but forty percent of the total would be retained by Chile to pay the indemnity owed her citizens. Under this arrangement, Bolivia actually received only thirty-five percent of the Arica custom house receipts. After the indemnities were paid, Bolivia had the right to move her custom house to her own territory and to transport goods across Chilean territory duty free.

Until the peace treaty was signed, Chile was to govern under her own laws and constitution the littoral between the twenty-third parallel and the mouth of the Loa River. The eastern boundary was to remain the same, the existing boundary in the Andes. The cession of this area did not become an issue because Bolivia was resigned to the fact that Chile would retain this territory as well as the rest of the province of Antofagasta. Chile regarded the area up to the Loa River as part of the province of Antofagasta. Bolivia did expect Chile to compensate her for the lost littoral with Tacna and Arica after Chile received them as the result of a favorable plebiscite at the end of the ten-year occupation.

Although two complementary protocols to the Pact of Truce were signed in April, 1884, and May, 1885, no significant changes in the truce terms were made. Some passages of the original pact were reworded for clarity; technical points concerning the custom house at Arica were included; prohibited items of commerce were listed; and the problem of upkeep on international roads and telegraph lines was settled. These points required attention before a peace treaty could be negotiated.

The Pact of Truce was designed as a temporary agreement to give both nations time to face the problems of peace making, but neither nation realized that a final treaty would not be signed for twenty years. One reason for the long delay was the problem of a port for Bolivia. Chile led Bolivia to believe that she would be compensated for the loss of Antofagasta by the acquisition of Tacna and Arica. Bolivia was willing to accept this exchange because Tacna and Arica had better ports with more direct access to the interior of Bolivia than her former littoral. Under article three of the Treaty of Ancón, Chile would gain sovereignty over Tacna and Arica only if she won the plebiscite to be held in 1894. The plebiscite was never held.

When the plebiscite was a year overdue, Bolivia insisted upon a definite peace treaty. On May 18, 1895, Chile and Bolivia signed a Treaty of Peace and Friendship. The general peace treaty was followed in a short time by several special treaties and protocols. [5] These agreements were not a final peace arrangement since they did not settle all the problems. Moreover, ratification of the treaty and special agreements was never exchanged. The terms of these agreements are indicative of the terms upon which the two nations could agree at that time. In the Treaty of Peace and Friendship Chilean sovereignty over the littoral was recognized in return for Chilean assumption of Bolivian debts to which the nitrates in the area were pledged. Bolivia was permitted to move her custom house to her own territory, and it was agreed that arbitration would settle any boundary disputes that might arise in the future. A Special Treaty on the Transference of Territory, which was signed at the same time, was to remain secret unless publication were agreed to by mutual consent. In the secret treaty Chile agreed to transfer Tacna and Arica to Bolivia if she gained sovereignty over them by plebiscite or by direct arrangement. Chile also pledged to employ every effort to acquire the provinces. In December of the same year a special protocol voided the absolute cession of Antofagasta by Bolivia if Chile failed to grant Bolivia a port within two years. The Treaty of Peace and Friendship in which Bolivia ceded Antofagasta to Chile, the Special Treaty on the Transference of Territory, and the special protocol of December which made the cession of the littoral conditional were to be considered one document. An additional protocol, signed April 30, 1896, attempted to settle specific points of disagreement on the cession of a port to Bolivia and the liquidation of Bolivian debts. It was hoped that the new protocol would expedite ratification of the earlier treaties and protocols. Although agreement was possible at the conference table, the governments involved refused their consent. All efforts for ratification failed, and both nations considered the series of agreements void.

In the ten year period since the end of hostilities, no progress toward a peace treaty had been made, and no further negotiations were attempted for an additional eight years. Finally, Bolivia decided that she could wait no longer for a solution. She could see no chance for Chile to settle the Tacna-Arica dispute with Peru. As long as Chile could not gain sovereignty over Tacna and Arica, there was no possibility of Bolivia's acquiring a seaport from a peace treaty with Chile; Bolivia decided to drop, for the time being, the discussion of a Pacific seaport and signed a Treaty of Peace and Friendship on October 20, 1904. [6] This treaty replaced the Pact of Truce signed twenty years earlier and formally established peace between the two nations. No mention was made of a seaport for Bolivia at that time or in the future, but provisions for transportation of Bolivian goods through Chilean territory were included. Free transit of goods to and from Bolivia was granted, and technical regulations for the transit of products, custom houses, and duties were agreed upon. Chile also agreed to build at her own expense a railroad from Arica to La Paz. The railroad was to be completed within one year from the date of the ratification of the peace treaty, and fifteen years after its completion that portion of the line in Bolivian territory would become the property of the Bolivian government. In addition, Chile would guarantee Bolivian loans not to exceed 1,700,000 pounds sterling for railroad construction between stated cities in Bolivia.

Article two of the treaty granted to Chile absolute and perpetual dominion in the Bolivian coastal province. Chile accepted the Bolivian financial obligations in the area and offered Bolivia an indemnity of 300,000 pounds sterling. The dispute over this area was one of the most important causes for the war. The treaty carefully stated the boundary of the area ceded by Bolivia, listing ninety-six points through which it ran. Six months after ratification a commission of engineers named by the two countries was to mark the boundary delineated in the treaty. If any differences remained unsettled after direct negotiations, the points in dispute would be referred to the Emperor of Germany for arbitration.

With the ratification of the treaty, the War of the Pacific officially ended, but not all of the problems were settled. The "question of the Pacific" remained an important factor in Bolivian politics as late as the decade of the 1930's and even today has not disappeared from Bolivian political discussions. As a result of the peace settlements Chile did gain possession of the nitrate deposits in Peru and Bolivia and consequently controlled the nitrate wealth which had played so important a part in causing the war. However, Chile also acquired the ill-will of Peru and Bolivia as well as other nations in Latin America and in Europe. Chile emerged from the War of the Pacific one of the three major powers in South America, but at the same time she gained the reputation of a greedy, ruthless country. This reputation, caused by her expansion to the north, was detrimental to Chile during the prolonged settlement of the Tacna-Arica dispute.

NOTES

1. Peruvian documents and Chilean decrees are printed in Ahumada Moreno, *Guerra del Pacifico*, 5.
2. Ahumada Moreno, *Guerra del Pacifico*, 6.
3. The Treaty of Ancón and documents relating to the Treaty of Ancón are printed in Ahumada Moreno, *Guerra del Pacifico*, 8.
4. The Pact of Truce and Protocols are printed in Ahumada Moreno, *Guerra del Pacifico*, 8, pp. 486-488.
5. Printed in Bascuñan Montes, *Recopilacion*, 3, pp. 282-301.
6. Bascuñan Montes, *Recopilacion*, 6, pp. 147-165.

CHAPTER 5. TACNA AND ARICA

THE Tacna-Arica dispute developed as a result of the failure of Chile and Peru to settle in the peace treaty the question of sovereignty over the two disputed provinces. Article three of the Treaty of Ancón provided for a plebiscite in March, 1894, under conditions to be agreed upon in subsequent negotiations. This special protocol, when concluded, was to be considered an integral part of the peace treaty. Immediately after the Treaty of Ancón was signed, Peru began discussions to find a basis for the plebiscite agreement. Although much correspondence was exchanged by the two governments, no progress was made until 1892. In August of that year the Peruvian minister of foreign affairs, E. Larrabure y Unanue, invited Javier Vial Solar, Chilean minister in Lima, to hold discussions to establish the basis for the special protocol. The proposal offered by Peru included the Chilean surrender of Tacna and Arica in exchange for commercial concessions from Peru. Since all communications received by Vial Solar were referred to Santiago for consideration, negotiations were extremely slow. It was not until April of 1893 that Chile finally rejected the Peruvian proposals. The first attempt to conclude the special protocol ended at that point.

Two more attempts were made to conclude the protocol, one in 1893 and the other early in 1894. Although very favorable commercial concessions were granted to Chile, especially in the 1893 discussions, both attempts failed because of Chilean cabinet crises. Parliamentary government had been established in Chile following the 1891 revolution against President José Balmaceda, and the failure of any party to achieve a majority necessitated coalition governments. Consequently, cabinet crises occurred regularly. The date for the plebiscite passed without any progress toward agreement on the special protocol. Peru considered it imperative that a plebiscite be held immediately. She regarded continued occupation by Chile as illegal, but even after further discussions were held in 1894, no agreement could be reached.

One explanation for the failure was the fact that Chile had no definite policy on Tacna and Arica. First she proposed that Peru sell her the provinces. When Peru refused, she insisted upon the plebiscite but would not agree upon conditions for holding it. In 1895 Chile signed a treaty with Bolivia in which she pledged to turn the provinces over to Bolivia if she gained sovereignty. Later she decided to retain them. There was no problem as far as Chile was concerned; therefore, she felt no pressing need to settle the question. Even though the ten year term stated in the Treaty of Ancón had expired, Chile retained possession of the area.

Not until 1898 did the two countries approach agreement. Because Chile was in imminent danger of becoming involved in a war with Argentina over ownership of Patagonia, sentiment in Chile favored a settlement of the Tacna-Arica question, and the government seemed disposed to compromise. During the war scare the Billinghurst-Latorre Protocol was drawn up and signed in April, 1898. The protocol provided that the suffrage requirement and the problem of a secret or public ballot should be submitted to the queen regent of Spain for arbitration. A plebiscite commission to which Spain, Peru, and Chile each would appoint one member was given the responsibility of registering voters and conducting the plebiscite. Other terms of the agreement provided for paying the expenses of the plebiscite and the ten million pesos indemnity to the loser of the plebiscite.

The Peruvian congress approved the protocol after a brief delay caused when some legislators questioned Chilean sincerity. The Chilean senate gave its approval and sent the agreement to the lower house. While the house was debating the document, an agreement was reached with Argentina submitting the Patagonian boundary question to arbitration by the queen of England. With the war scare over, the pressure to come to terms with Peru ended. After protracted debate, the Chilean house refused to approve the protocol but did not definitely reject it. Discussion of the protocol was indefinitely postponed. Almost two years later, in January of 1901, the House of Deputies rejected the protocol and returned it to the executive for further negotiations. The house expressed an unwillingness to submit the points in dispute to arbitration and stated a preference for direct negotiations instead.

During the two year period the Billinghurst-Latorre Protocol was pending before the Chilean house, Peru continued to negotiate on the basis of that agreement. By the time the protocol was finally rejected by Chile, relations had become strained to the breaking point. Peru protested the Chilean attempt to Chileanize the provinces of Tacna and Arica in order to obtain a favorable vote if a plebiscite were held. These protest remained unanswered. Furthermore, Peru felt that her diplomatic representative had been ill-treated by the Chilean government, and she decided to recall her minister in Santiago. In the second week of March, 1901, Minister Cesáreo Chacaltana requested an audience with President Federico Errázuriz Echaurren to present his letter of recall. Shortly before Chacaltana's recall, the Chilean minister in Lima, who had been granted a leave of absence, had returned to Chile; so diplomatic relations were suspended until November, 1905, when Peru appointed a new minister to Chile.

Both countries expressed a desire to open negotiations immediately. However, almost three years passed before a start was made in March, 1908. In the ensuing discussions Chile attempted to include points of common interest unrelated to the plebiscite. Chile wanted to include conventions reducing customs on the products of each country consumed in the other, pooling resources for construction of a railroad between Lima and Santiago, and increasing the ten million peso indemnity stipulated in the Treaty of Ancón. Peru not only rejected the proposal to link other matters to the plebiscite discussions, but she also considered Chilean terms for holding the plebiscite unsatisfactory. The Chilean conditions would have given Chilean citizens and foreigners as well as Peruvian citizens residing in the disputed area the right to vote. Chile also claimed the exclusive right to appoint the officials to preside over the plebiscite, to count the vote, and to announce the results. Although discussions continued for two years, no progress was made. Chile seemed satisfied to permit the dispute to continue if she could not get Peru to agree to her terms. The continuing Chileanization of the disputed area, an official policy of the Chilean government, led Peru to sever diplomatic relations in March, 1910.

Although formal relations were not resumed, negotiations began again in 1912 with an exchange of telegrams between the foreign ministers of the two nations. A tentative agreement known as the Valera-Huneeus Protocol was concluded in November of that year.[1] The terms of the new agreement included the re-establishment of diplomatic relations, a reciprocal trade treaty, and an agreement to hold the Tacna-Arica plebiscite twenty-one years from the date of the signing of this protocol. The Valera-Huneeus Protocol further stipulated that the plebiscite protocol when written should limit the right to vote in the plebiscite to Peruvians and Chileans who could read and write and who had resided in the area for three years before the election. The plebiscite protocol was also to provide for an election board composed of five members, two chosen by the Peruvian government and two chosen by the Chilean government. The President of the Supreme Court of Chile would serve as the chairman of the election board with a deciding vote in case of a tie. All decisions of the board would be binding upon both nations. The indemnity provided for in the Treaty of Ancón would be paid in full by the nation gaining possession of the provinces.

When President Guillermo Billinghurst presented the Valera-Huneeus Protocol to the Peruvian congress for approval, there was a violent outburst of public opinion against the government. The public reaction to this treaty was a factor in his removal from office in 1914. President Billinghurst defended the agreement, arguing that it made definite provisions for the plebiscite to be held within a stated period. Furthermore, Chile, by signing this agreement, recognized her possession of the area as a temporary occupation rather than sovereignty. The main point in his statement to congress was an intimation that since Chile would never fulfill any agreement carrying out the Treaty of Ancón, the twenty-one year delay would give Peru time to prepare militarily for a final settlement. Upon learning of President Billinghurst's message to congress, Chile rejected the agreement. The Peruvian congress had already tabled the protocol.

The controversy remained dormant during World War I, but the organization of the League of Nations after the war gave Peru an opportunity to bring public opinion to bear upon Chile. In 1920 Peru submitted the Tacna-Arica question to the League. The secretary-general informed Peru that the request had been received too late to be included on the agenda for that year. Nevertheless, Chile immediately challenged the request. The League, choosing to consider the dispute an internal American affair that should be handled by the American nations, was reluctant to discuss the Tacna-Arica question. Peru withdrew her request at the end of the year.

During the same year, Chile initiated another attempt to reach a settlement based upon the Valera-Huneeus proposals. Peru refused to accept those terms and, as a counterproposal, suggested arbitration by the United States. Arbitration was acceptable to Chile, but the two nations could not agree upon the differences to be submitted to the arbitrator. At that point the United States invited the two countries to send representatives to Washington, D. C., to settle their differences concerning the arrangements for arbitration. Both nations accepted the invitation and appointed special delegates. Carlos Aldunate and Luiz Izguierdo represented Chile; Carlos F. Porras and Hernán Velarde represented Peru.

Secretary of State Charles Evans Hughes opened the first session on May 15, 1922, with a welcoming address that praised the conciliatory spirit of both nations and expressed the hope that a satisfactory settlement could be found. Peru was not as hopeful. Sr. Porras, chairman of Peruvian delegation, presented the views of his country.[2] The only just solution was the restoration of the provinces to Peru. Because of Chile's refusal to conclude the special protocol stipulated by the Treaty of Ancón, the plebiscite had not been held twenty-eight years after the expiration of the ten year period. Furthermore, information obtained from Chilean authorities proved that in 1894 the majority of Tacna and Arica citizens were Peruvian. Peru was justified in assuming that a virtual plebiscite, the results of which were favorable to Peru, had taken place. Consequently, the only solution fulfilling the third article of the Treaty of Ancón was to accept the 1894 decision of the provinces to return to Peru. Realizing that Chile would not accept these statements, Sr. Porras proposed arbitration and submitted the following items as the basis for discussion:

> The question of whether the plebiscite should be held under existing conditions would be submitted to arbitration.
> If the plebiscite were not held the question of sovereignty would be submitted to arbitration.
> If the plebiscite were held the conditions for holding it would be submitted to arbitration.

Chile maintained that the Peruvian proposal could not be considered since it had the effect of nullifying article three of the Treaty of Ancón. [3] The terms on which this conference had been called limited the discussions to fulfilling the unfulfilled portions of that treaty. Chile then offered a four point counterproposal as the basis for arbitration. Chile suggested the Valera-Huneeus negotiations of 1912 or a 1909 Chilean proposal which Peru had already rejected. The other part of the Chilean proposal offered arbitration of all points upon which no prior agreements had been reached or new negotiations without reference to previous discussions. Any differences arising out of the new negotiations would be submitted to arbitration.

Peruvian refusal to accept the Chilean proposals deadlocked the conference until Secretary Hughes intervened. After informal discussions with both delegations, Mr. Hughes suggested an agreement acceptable to both nations. On June 20, 1922, the delegates signed a Protocol of Arbitration which submitted the questions arising from the unfulfilled stipulations of article three of the Treaty of Ancón to the arbitration of the President of the United States. [4] A supplementary act signed the same day and considered an integral part of the protocol made it virtually impossible for the arbitrator to do anything except try to hold the plebiscite. If the President decided against the plebiscite, the problem would be sent back to the two countries for further discussion. If the arbitrator decided that the plebiscite should be held, he was authorized to determine the conditions for conducting it. The question of the northern and southern boundaries, the Tarata and Chilcayo areas, was included in the arbitration by the supplementary act.

In the middle of January of the following year, the Protocol and the Supplementary Act were ratified, and two weeks later the President of the United States accepted the position as arbitrator. By March agreement had been reached on the procedure and date for presentation of the cases and countercases of both nations. In November Peru presented her case. She maintained that she should be granted ownership of the provinces not only because Chilean policy had prevented the Tacna-Arica plebiscite from being held in the past but also because Chilean policy had created conditions in the provinces which prevented a just plebiscite in the future. To prove her case Peru summarized the causes and conduct of the War of the Pacific and the peace negotiations. There followed a detailed description of the negotiations in which Peru had attempted to determine the conditions for the plebiscite. Peru then cited examples of the Chileanization of the provinces which had changed conditions so much that a plebiscite should not be held. She ended her case with a request that the arbitrator rule against holding a plebiscite and that he immediately grant Peru unencumbered sovereignty over the area.

Chile in her case maintained that the only question before the arbitrator was whether under the existing circumstances the plebiscite should or should not be held. If he decided in the affirmative, he must determine the conditions. If he decided in the negative, his duties as arbitrator ended, and the question reverted to the two parties. Any discussion of the causes of the war, of the war itself, or of the peace terms was beyond the scope of the arbitration. In addition, Chile contended that the plebiscite was never held because the two nations could not agree upon the conditions under which it would be conducted. She requested the arbitrator to decide in favor of the plebiscite and to determine the procedures for holding it.

President Calvin Coolidge handed down the opinion and award of the arbitrator on March 4, 1925. He decided in favor of the plebiscite. In the opinion of the arbitrator the terms of the Treaty of Ancón were still in force. Although the treaty stated that the plebiscite could not be held until ten years after ratification, it did not fix any limit to the period of time in which the plebiscite must be conducted or the special protocol signed. President Coolidge also refused to blame Chile entirely for the failure to agree upon the protocol. In response to the Peruvian charges of Chileanization, the arbitrator expressed disapproval of Chile's administration of the provinces and her treatment of Peruvian citizens. However, he held that the Chilean administration was not a barrier to holding the plebiscite because conditions suitable for safeguarding the interest of both nations could be established.

The award had been described as more of a political than a judi-

66

cial decision. Chile was chided in order to placate Peru but not strongly enough to alienate Chile. The decision to hold the plebiscite was decided by one consideration. Failure to hold the plebiscite would return the whole question to direct settlement by Chile and Peru, and for forty-one years those negotiations had been unsuccessful. President Coolidge felt that if the United States supervised the plebiscite it would be conducted under conditions just to both nations.

After deciding in favor of the plebiscite, the arbitrator had to determine the conditions under which it would be held. The first problem was to define the electorate. Voting privileges were limited with some exceptions to male persons, twenty-one years of age, who could read and write and who qualified under one of the following three conditions: persons born in Tacna-Arica; Chileans and Peruvians who had resided continuously in the territory from July 20, 1922, the date of the Protocol of Arbitration, to the date of voter registration; or persons, neither Peruvian nor Chilean, who were qualified for naturalization in the state winning the plebiscite. No owner of real property in the area was to be disfranchised because of his inability to read or write. No person who was or had ever been a member of the armed service, police, or government of either country could vote unless he had been born in the provinces. The usual restrictions, such as insanity or criminal conviction, were also applied. General rules for conducting the election were outlined, but the right to administer the plebiscite, to register voters, and to appoint election boards was granted to a commission of three members. This commission was to have complete control of the plebiscite, but the arbitrator reserved the right to hear appeals from the commission.

The last question before the arbitrator was the boundaries of the area. The northern boundary was quickly settled. Only the provinces of Tacna and Arica were included in the plebiscite because the Peruvian province of Tarata was not mentioned in the Treaty of Ancon. The portion of Tarata that Chile had included in Tacna was returned to Peru. The southern boundary was more difficult to determine; it ran through the Chilcaya area which contained valuable borax fields. President Coolidge decided that the boundary should remain the same as the Peruvian provincial boundary of October 20, 1883, the date of the Treaty of Ancon. Because this line could not definitely be marked, the President reserved the right to appoint at a later date a special commission to determine the boundary line.

In his capacity as arbitrator President Coolidge appointed General John J. Pershing president of the plebiscite commission on March 23, 1925. Shortly afterward, Chile named Augustin Edwards, but Peru did not name her representative, Manuel de Freyre Santander, until June. The commission's opening session, which took place in Arica, was not held until the end of August. Peru had reservations from the beginning. She was sure that a fair plebiscite could not be held unless she were granted certain guarantees considered unnecessary by the arbitrator. In the first session of the commission both Chile and Peru charged the other nation with acts designed to nullify the results of the plebiscite. Chile accused Peru of delaying registration and voting in the arbitration commission in a way calculated to postpone the plebiscite indefinitely. Acts of violence against Peruvians, including members of the official delegation, led Peru to charge that the policy of Chileanization was still in effect to the extent that Peruvian citizens were being forced to leave the area or to refrain from registering.

The fact that General Pershing found it necessary to issue guarantees to ensure a free plebiscite substantiates the Peruvian charges. The commission took up the issue, but while the question was being discussed, Sr. Edwards withdrew from the deliberations at the request of his government. Then Chile sent a message to the commission demanding that registration begin on December 20 and that the election be conducted on February 1, 1926. The same note charged General Pershing with favoring Peru. Three weeks later the commission passed a resolution severely censuring the Chilean authorities in Tacna and Arica. The resolution of censure stated that Chile had prevented progress toward the plebiscite and had unlawfully expelled or intimidated Peruvian citizens. The resolution further stated that if Chile continued to absent herself from the meetings of the commission no plebiscite could be conducted and the commission would be required to report to the arbitrator that the failure was due to Chilean actions. The resolution concluded with a schedule. Registration would begin on February 15, 1926, and voting would take place on April 15 or as soon thereafter as possible. The dates depended upon the cooperation of both parties.

Later in December, the United States Department of State confirmed the rumor that General Pershing was leaving the plebiscite commission because of ill health. At the end of January, 1926, General William Lassiter, commander of the military forces in the Canal Zone, replaced General Pershing, who had returned to the United States for dental treatment. Before General Pershing left, the electoral law had been approved by the plebiscite commission, but it was not promulgated until February 15. Because of the delay it was necessary to change the registration and voting dates from February 15 and April 15 to March 27 and April 27.

One week before registration was to start, both Chile and Peru appealed the commission's decision on voting qualifications to the arbitrator.

President Coolidge upheld the commission. Two weeks later Peru demanded that the date for registration be postponed indefinitely because Peruvian voters had insufficient protection. Meanwhile, the United States Department of State extended its good offices to settle the dispute without the plebiscite. Both disputants accepted; but Chile insisted that the plebiscite proceedings continue, and Peru wanted them canceled. When registration began Peruvian voters, following instructions from the Peruvian member of the plebiscite commission, refused to register. At that point negotiations were transferred to Washington.

Two months after the Washington discussions had started, the report of the plebiscite commission was published. The Lassiter report criticized the Chilean government for failure to maintain sufficient order for conducting a plebiscite and recommended the abandonment of the plebiscite. The commission ended its report by blaming the Chilean government for the termination of the plebiscite proceedings. Chile objected violently to the commission report, but she continued to take part in the Washington negotiations throughout the remainder of the year and into 1927.

The United States offered several solutions to the problem. Among the most widely discussed were proposals to divide the area between Peru and Chile, to neutralize the territory, or to give the provinces to Bolivia in order to provide her with a seacoast. Bolivia readily accepted the last proposal. She had been trying to obtain the area since before the War of the Pacific. Chile also accepted this proposal, but Peru refused to consider it. It seemed to Peru that she was the one required to make a sacrifice. The area was Peruvian not Chilean, and Chile had nothing to lose by relinquishing it.

All of the proposals submitted by the United States were rejected by one or both nations, but they did agree to discuss them further. Certain parts of the proposals were acceptable to each. In the course of the sessions it became evident that Chile was mainly concerned about a safe and fixed northern boundary. She feared that Peru would attempt to regain Tarapacá, the rich nitrate province, if Tacna and Arica were returned. Peru, on the other hand, was demanding the return of Tacna in order to save national pride. During the two years that the Washington discussions were being held, the necessity for settling the dispute became more evident. When Chile was blamed for the failure to hold the plebiscite, she was placed in the position of having violated the Treaty of Ancon. Her violation of the treaty raised legal doubt about her possession of not only Tacna-Arica but also Tarapaca. Economic conditions in both countries made an expensive arms race impractical. The profits from nitrates declined so drastically after World War I that the area no longer had its former economic importance. These developments made Chile more willing to compromise.

In July, 1928, diplomatic and commercial relations between Chile and Peru, severed in 1910, were resumed through the diplomatic efforts of Secretary of State Frank B. Kellogg. When ambassadors were exchanged in October, direct negotiations replaced the Washington conferences and resulted in the Treaty of Santiago with a complementary protocol, both signed in Lima on June 3, 1929, and ratified the following month. Article one of the treaty declared the dispute originated by article three of the Treaty of Ancón solved. The disputed area was divided; Tacna was given to Peru and Arica to Chile. It was agreed that the boundary between the two nations should be a line approximately ten kilometers north of and parallel to the Arica-La Paz railroad. Thirty days after the ratification of the treaty, Chile was to deliver Tacna to Peru. Peru was also to be paid an indemnity of six million pesos for her loss of Arica. The children of Peruvians in Arica were to be considered Peruvian until they reached twenty-one years of age at which time they could choose their nationality. Chileans in Tacna were to have the same right. An additional paragraph in the treaty provided that a memorial to commemorate peace between the two nations would be erected on the Morro of Arica.

In the protocol the two states pledged that neither would cede any part of the territory included in this settlement to a third state without having first gained the consent of the other. This provision also required the agreement of both for the construction of new international railroads by either state. Another clause in the protocol guaranteed Peru free transit across Arica. The only existing railroad in Tacna and Arica was the Arica-La Paz railroad. In the final section, Chile assumed the cost of erecting the peace memorial and promised to keep the Morro of Arica free of armaments.

A peaceful solution to the territorial problem arising from the War of the Pacific had finally been reached. Chile received her fixed and safe northern boundary, and Peru obtained the return of Tacna. The restoration of peaceful relations resulted in economic benefits for both. For thirty-five years the Tacna-Arica problem had disrupted friendly relations between Peru and Chile and at times had threatened to lead to war. The rapprochement brought about by the efforts of the United States resulted in the solution of one of the most vexing boundary problems in Latin America.

NOTES

1. See Arbitration Between Peru and Chile: Appendix to the Case of Peru
   in the Matter of the Controversy arising out of the Question of the
   Pacific before the President of the United States Arbitrator under
   the Protocol and supplementary Act between the Republic of Peru
   and the Republic of Chile, signed July 20, 1922, at Washington,
   D. C., ratified January 15, 1923 (Washington, D. C., 1923).
2. For the Peruvian Case see Arbitration Between Peru and Chile: The
   Case of Peru in the Matter of the Controversy arising out of the
   Question of the Pacific before the President of the United States
   Arbitrator under the Protocol and supplementary Act between the
   Republic of Peru and the Republic of Chile, signed July 20, 1922,
   at Washington, D. C., ratified January 15, 1923 (Washington, D. C.,
   1923).
   Arbitration Between Peru and Chile: Appendix to the Case of Peru...
   (Washington, D. C., 1923).
   Arbitration Between Peru and Chile: The Counter Case of Peru...
   (Washington, D. C., 1923).
   Arbitration Between Peru and Chile: Appendix to the Counter Case
   of Peru...(Washington, D. C., 1923).
   Arbitration Between Peru and Chile: The Memorial of Peru and the
   Ruling and Observations of the Arbitrator (In English and Spanish)
   (Washington, D. C., 1925).
3. For the Chilean Case see Tacna-Arica Arbitration: The Case of the
   Republic of Chile submitted to the President of the United States as
   Arbitrator under the Provisions of the Protocol and Supplementary
   Agreement Entered Into Between Chile and Peru at Washington on
   July 20, 1922 (Washington, D. C., 1923).
   Tacna-Arica Arbitration: Appendix to the Case of Chile...(Wash-
   ington, D. C., 1923).
   Tacna-Arica Arbitration: The Counter Case of Chile...(Washing-
   ton, D. C., 1924).
   Tacna-Arica Arbitration: Appendix to the Counter Case of Chile...
   (Washington, D. C., 1924).
   Tacna-Arica Arbitration: Notes on the Peruvian Case and Appen-
   dix submitted with the Counter-Case of the Republic of Chile to the
   President...(Washington, D. C., 1924).
4. In the Matter of the Arbitration Between the Republic of Chile and the
   Republic of Peru, with regard to the unfulfilled Provisions of the

Treaty of Peace of October 20, 1883, under the Protocol and Supplementary Act Signed at Washington July 20, 1922, Opinion and Award of the Arbitrator (Washington, D. C. , 1925).

5. William Jefferson Dennis, *Documentary History of the Tacna-Arica Dispute*, University of Iowa Studies in the Social Sciences, 8, pp. 316-320.

CHAPTER 6. THE STRAIT OF MAGELLAN

THE eastern boundary separating Chile and Argentina, like the
northern boundary in the Desert of Atacama, was unknown in certain
areas and unmarked along its entire extent. Only in general terms did
Chile define this boundary in any of her constitutions or decrees adopted
during the first years of independence. The usual description is from the
Desert of Atacama to Cape Horn and from the Pacific Ocean to the Cordillera of the Andes. Since natural obstacles such as deserts or mountains
separated Chile from neighboring countries and the frontiers were uninhabited except by Indians, there seemed to be no need for a precise definition of the boundary.

However, a dispute with Argentina did arise over the eastern boundary about the same time the controversy arose over the northern frontier.
The discovery of mineral wealth in the Desert of Atacama during the decade
of the 1830's led to the expansion northward that culminated in the War of
the Pacific and the extension of Chilean territory. In the same decade,
events occurred that resulted in Chile's moving into the Strait of Magellan
area. During the 1830's Chilean interest in the Strait of Magellan was
aroused by English activity there. Although the British government did
not officially consider colonizing the region, it displayed an interest which
caused concern in Chile. The two voyages of the Adventure and the Beagle
seemed to Chile to constitute a threat to her sovereignty over the territory
in the Strait area. In May, 1826, the British admiralty ordered a survey
of Tierra del Fuego and of South America from the southern entrance of
the Río de la Plata to Chiloé.[1] Two surveying vessels, the Adventure under the command of Captain Philip Parker King and the Beagle under the
command of Captain Pringle Stokes, sailed from Plymouth on May 22, 1826,
on the first voyage. After stopping at various points en route to make observations of longitude, the expedition proceeded to the Río de la Plata and
entered Montevideo harbor on October 13. About a month later they began
the survey of the coast southward to the Strait of Magellan, which they entered on December 28, 1826. For almost three years the ships stayed in

73

the Strait, exploring, surveying, and mapping. During this time it was necessary to return occasionally to Buenos Aires or Montevideo for supplies and repairs. While the Beagle was in Montevideo to refit in October, 1828, Captain Robert Fitz Roy took over her command, replacing Captain Stokes, who had died in August after shooting himself "in a fit of despondency."[2] Captain Fitz Roy remained in command during the remainder of the first voyage and throughout the second voyage.

In 1829 the expedition extended the survey into Chilean territory, from the western end of the Strait northward to Chiloé. After obtaining repairs and supplies at Chiloé, the Beagle sailed south once again, this time sailing around the southern coast of Tierra del Fuego. The Adventure, however, remained in Chilean waters courting Chilean favor and good will. Captain King paid an official call on Supreme Director Antonio Pinto to explain the purpose of the voyage and to obtain the cooperation of the Chilean government. The English ship left Chile in the middle of March, 1830, met the Beagle in the Strait, and returned with her sister ship to Rio de Janeiro. In August both ships sailed for England, completing the first surveying expedition in October, 1830.

The Beagle left England on her second voyage to South America late in December, 1831. She carried instructions to complete the survey of the southern coast of South America, to return the Fuegians taken to England on the first voyage, and to obtain the meridian distance across the Pacific Ocean on her return trip. Since it was deemed advisable to have a man with scientific education to collect and classify specimens of the flora and fauna of the area, Charles Darwin was included in the Beagle's crew as volunteer naturalist. It was on this voyage that Darwin collected much information he later used in his work, The Origin of Species. While on this voyage Darwin kept a journal, which is volume three of the account of the voyages of the Adventure and the Beagle.

Until July, 1832, the Beagle was engaged in making observations in the Atlantic and along the Brazilian coast; in August she began the survey of the Atlantic coast of Argentina. Leaving a small crew to complete this survey, she sailed to Tierra del Fuego in December. The three Fuegians being returned to their homeland were landed on Navarin Island, but an attempt to establish a mission there proved futile. The Beagle remained in the area surveying Tierra del Fuego until February, 1833, when she sailed on to survey the Falkland Islands.

In the preceding month H. M. S. Clio and H. M. S. Tyne had reasserted British sovereignty over the Falkland Islands. The British had voluntarily surrendered control in 1774, after which Spain claimed exclusive jurisdiction. Following independence, Argentina assumed the Spanish

74

claim to the Malvinas Islands, as she called them, and occupied them in 1820. When British sovereignty was again asserted on January 2, 1833, the Argentine authorities were forced to return to Buenos Aires. Argentina refused to recognize British sovereignty and still claims the islands.

While in the Falkland Islands Captian Fitz Roy purchased a smaller, auxiliary ship, which he renamed the Adventure. The second vessel was used as a tender to obtain supplies, enabling the Beagle to devote full time to surveying. In April Captain Fitz Roy ordered the Beagle to Montevideo for extensive repairs and supplies. It was not until December that the Beagle and her tender were able to leave Montevideo. The two ships sailed south again to the Falkland Islands, stopping at Port San Julian to complete the survey of that area and at Navarino Island to inquire into the fate of the Fuegians left there the year before. The Indians had reverted almost completely to their former life.

When Captain Fitz Roy reached the Falkland Islands on March 10, 1834, he found the British lieutenant, four seamen, and six marines who had been left to govern the islands attempting to subdue a small band of lawless gauchos that had murdered five colonists, one of whom was the representative of the British government. The Beagle's crew provided assistance, and law and order were restored. England has exercised sovereignty over the Falkland Islands continuously since 1833 by right of discovery and occupation, but Argentina maintains that her claim is superior because she controlled and occupied the islands before the British. In 1833 and 1834 Chile saw the Falklands as an example of British colonial expansion which she feared the Beagle voyages would extend into the Strait.

Nevertheless, when the Beagle arrived in Chiloé in June, 1834, the Chilean government granted the expedition permission to make a survey of the Chilean coast the following spring. A small party remained to chart the northern ports of Chile when the Beagle sailed from Peru to the Galápagos Islands and from there across the Pacific on her return voyage to England. Captain Fitz Roy and his crew anchored at Falmouth in October, 1836, after a voyage of four years and nine months.

The interest in the Strait area that the voyages for the survey of the Strait had incited in Europe, especially in England and France, and in Chile was intensified by the publication in 1839 of the account of the voyages. These three volumes not only gave an accurate description of the area but also contained suggestions relating to the potentialities and possible uses of the area. Captain Fitz Roy, for instance, considered the Strait desirable for colonization and felt that with the Falkland Islands the Strait could provide ports of call for sealers in the South Atlantic and for vessels using the Pacific route between England and Australia. All such

75

statements seemed to Chile a clear indication that her suspicion about English intentions was well founded.

The belief that England had designs on the Strait was confirmed for many Chileans in 1840 by an incident that took place in the Strait. Five years before, William Wheelwright, a North American engineer active in South American railroad construction, had obtained from the Chilean government the exclusive right for a steamship line between Chilean and Peruvian ports.[3] He organized in England the Pacific Steam Navigation Company, which purchased two steamships to be built in England. On September 14, 1840, the two ships, the Chile and the Peru, entered the Strait of Magellan on their maiden voyage from England to Chile. When the ships stopped at Port Hunger for five days to obtain water and wood, Captain George Peacock, commander of the squadron, organized a ceremony to commemorate Chilean Independence Day, September 18. The passengers and crew formed two lines in the plaza. At the front of the column a small English flag was carried, and in the center of the column a large Chilean flag was displayed. The company marched to the heights of Point Santa Ana and erected a buoy twenty-five feet high. A document containing information about this first voyage of steam vessels through the Strait was deposited at the foot of the buoy along with an English coin which carried the portrait of Queen Victoria. The Chilean flag was planted at the top of the buoy and saluted by the company and by the guns of the ships. The next day the Chilean flag was removed, and the squadron continued the voyage. The account of the ceremony circulated in Chile contained only a portion of the whole celebration. Chileans knew the English flag had been carried ashore and that a coin with the likeness of Queen Victoria and a document had been buried.

Actually, Chile had less to fear from England than from France. French expeditions, sponsored by the government or private individuals, had aroused interest in the Strait of Magellan and in some cases had resulted in plans for French colonization of the area. The first of these expeditions was a private undertaking headed by Captain Duhaut-Ally who passed through the Strait in August of 1826 on a voyage around the world. Captain Duhaut-Ally published a book about his voyage in which he expressed enthusiasm for French colonization of the Strait. He also presented a memorial to the Minister of Marine recommending colonization.

Duhaut-Ally was followed by Admiral Abel Aubert Dupetit-Thouars who sailed from Toulon in January, 1832, on a two year voyage of circumnavigation. Upon his return he urged his government to establish colonies in the Pacific islands before England could claim all of them. England had just occupied New Zealand. In 1841 Admiral Dupetit-Thouars sailed from

Brest to the Pacific where he proclaimed the French Protectorate over Tahiti and occupied the Mariana Islands. He expressed a desire to see a French colony in the Strait of Magellan to serve as a way station to colonies in the Pacific.

Another French Captain, Jules Sébastien César Dumont D'urville, on a polar expedition sponsored by his government in 1837 made a prolonged visit to Port Famine before he discovered the portion of Antarctica he named Louis Philippe. Upon his return to France in 1840, Dumont D'Urville, who had been promoted to the rank of admiral for his service, formally proposed to his government a project for the colonization of the Strait of Magellan "not only as a means of extending the influence of France but as a civilizing work useful for the commerce of the world."[4] Even the death of the Admiral did not stop his plan. Vincendon Damoulin, the engineer-geographer on the expedition, continued to work for it, and many members expressed their approval when the Chamber of Deputies considered the project. Although the active interest of the French government in colonization of the area made the French a much greater threat to Chilean control of the Strait than the English, Chile was not as acutely aware of the French activity. Enough was known about the French threat to cause some official concern, but not enough to arouse any public protest.

Before the era of British and French activity in the Strait, a few Chileans, including Bernardo O'Higgins, had tried to interest the Chilean government in expansion into the area. While in exile in Peru, O'Higgins corresponded with men in England and Chile about establishing a company to operate steam tugs for towing sailing ships through the Strait. He also proposed the founding of a colony to effect Chilean control. O'Higgins communicated with the Chilean minister of state on these projects, but he was not able to interest the Chilean government. Not until 1842 did Chile take steps to extend her active supervision to the area.

Toward the end of 1841 George Mabon, a North American lobster fisherman familiar with the Strait and the surrounding area, petitioned the Chilean government for a ten year concession granting him the right to operate steam tugs in the Strait.[5] By the decree of December 21, 1841, a special commission composed of Diego Antonio Barros, Santiago Ingran, and Domingo Espiñeira was set up to determine the feasibility of the project. The commission approved the idea but decided it was necessary first to establish effective as well as theoretic sovereignty over the area. Mabon's petition was pigeonholed, and he had to wait a year before he learned the finding of the special committee.

During that year plans for sending an expedition to the Strait of Magellan were being made. Espiñeira, one of the members of the special

77

commission, was appointed Intendant of Chiloé on April 1, 1842. He arrived in San Carlos de Ancud to assume his duties in the middle of the month. The new intendant carried instructions from Manuel Montt, interim Minister of War and Marine. Intendant Espiñeira was ordered to gather information about suitable sites for colonies on the coast of the Strait of Magellan from people in Chiloé who had been to the Strait. If these people gave discouraging reports, the intendant was instructed to organize an exploratory expedition under the leadership of an able man who would be advised by someone experienced in the founding and sustaining of colonies. The instructions further specified that the intendant was to send an expedition during the most favorable season, taking into account the practice of the Indians on their fishing voyages to the vicinity of the Strait. He was also told to keep an account of expenses so that he might be reimbursed and to forward all information obtained by the expedition to the government as soon as possible.

Before assuming his duties in Chiloe, Intendant Espiñeira had heard that William Low had more complete information about the Strait than any other individual. Low had been engaged in whaling, sealing, and lobster fishing in and around the Strait for thirty years. On the Beagle's second voyage Captain Fitz Roy had purchased the tender which he renamed the Adventure from Low and later had written to the British Admiralty that this man possessed more general and navigational information about the Falkland Islands, Tierra del Fuego, Patagonia, and the Galápagos Islands than any other individual without exception. Unfortunately, William Low had died in Chiloé six months before the arrival of Espiñeira. Because Low was the main source of information useful for colonization of the Strait, it was now necessary to send an expedition to the area.

One of the first problems Espiñeira faced was that of obtaining a ship for the expedition. The Chilean navy in 1842 consisted of a frigate and two armed schooners. The schooners were used in the coastal service, and the frigate Chile was assigned to the naval school as a training ship. Since the Minister of Marine had no vessel which he could assign to the expedition going to the Strait, he authorized Espiñeira to construct a ship in Chiloé. [6]

Espiñeira placed John Williams, Captain of the Port of San Carlos, in charge of building the ship and in command of the expedition. John Williams or Juan Guillermos as he called himself in Chile was born in 1798 in Bristol, England. He had learned the art of navigation from his father in ships of the East Indies Company. At the time of the fight for independence in South America, Williams took service with Peru. In 1824 he enlisted as an officer in the Chilean navy, seeing service on the Galvarino and Juana

78

Pastora. He assisted in the Chiloé campaign, and in 1830 he received a promotion to capitán de corbeta and the post of Captain of the Port of San Carlos. During the rebellion of Ramón Freire, he fought against the government and was captured with Freire in August of 1836. Williams was imprisoned and separated from the navy for political reasons, but he was reinstated in his rank and restored to duty during the Peruvian-Bolivian Confederation campaign. In June of 1839 Williams was in command of the frigate Monteagudo, which was docked in Valparaiso after a voyage from Callao, Peru. A storm broke the moorings and drove the ship on the rocks. Williams, who was on land at the time, was seriously injured when the shallop in which he was attempting to return to his ship was dashed against the wharf by a wave. During his convalescence, he requested and received his former post as Captain of the Port of San Carlos de Ancud, and that was his position at the time the expedition to the Strait of Magellan was being organized.

The ship for the expedition was constructed in an improvised dockyard in San Carlos. The ship, a schooner of war, was forty feet long, eight and one-half feet wide, and four feet deep in the hold. She was built at a cost of 1,457.03 pesos. This amount included the cost of bringing such naval supplies as sails, ropes, and anchors from Valparaiso. Although the schooner was scheduled to be ready in October, 1842, a change in her design to accommodate thirty persons aboard delayed her completion until February of the following year. At first the name Bulnes in honor of the president was chosen, but when President Manuel Bulnes declined the honor, the schooner was named the Ancud.

Seven months provisions, consisting mainly of jerked beef, beans, and hardtack, were taken aboard for twenty-one people. In addition the schooner carried an ample supply of tobacco, liquor, and wine, including one hundred and ten gallons of aguardiente, one barrel of smooth wine, one case of twenty-four bottles of San Vicente wine, and six gallons of rum. The only medical supplies on board were two bottles of palma christi and two pounds of Epsom salts. However, some of the liquor was occasionally used for medicine.

The crew of nine included John Williams as commander; George Mabon, the man who petitioned for the tugboat concession, as pilot; Ricardo Didimus as helmsman; and six sailors. The garrison for the fort which was to be built in the Strait was commanded by Lieutenant of Artillery Manuel González Hidalgo followed in descending rank by Second Sergeant Eusebio Pizarro, Corporal José Hidalgo, and five soldiers. The remaining persons aboard were the volunteer naturalist, Bernardo Eunom Philippi; a carpenter; the cabin boy, Horacio Luis Williams, second son of the commander; and two women who were wives of soldiers in the garrison. A total of twenty-two persons made up this expedition to colonize the Strait of Magellan.

The volunteer naturalist, Philippi, was born in Charlottenburg, Prussia. [7] He studied at the Pestalozzi school in French Switzerland and later in Berlin at the Grey Convent and the Realschule. Upon completion of his education, Philippi entered the corps of engineers. After fulfilling his military obligation, he served aboard merchant ships before attending naval school where he received the rating of pilot. Soon after receiving his pilot's rating, Philippi went to Chile on a merchant ship and decided to remain in that country to gather material for a natural history of the area. He returned to Prussia in 1840 and persuaded the government to send him to Chile as a naturalist. His hope of making his study commercially profitable failed, but he learned a great deal about Peru and Chiloé. It was in Chiloé that Philippi first met Williams and Espiñeira and learned about the Strait expedition. After financing his work for one year, the Prussian government failed to send money for a second year's work. When the money for further work did not arrive, Philippi obtained permission from the government of Chile to accompany the Strait expedition, in which he had become interested during his visit to Chiloé.

When he returned from the Strait, Philippi was commissioned captain of engineers in the Chilean army. He soon became interested in German colonization of the area around Valdivia. This interest led him to join the German consul in forming a company which was responsible for the beginning of German immigration. His immigration activities were supported by President Bulnes, who promoted him to lieutenant colonel and sent him to Germany to further the project. The Revolutions of 1848 helped make Philippi's work much easier; large numbers of Germans escaped unsettled conditions at home by going to Chile. Because the Bishops of Paderbon and Fulda opposed any migration from their bishoprics, they told the Chilean bishops that more Protestants than Catholics were going to Chile. Pressure from the Chilean bishops forced the recall of Philippi. President Manuel Montt then named him Governor of the Colony of Magellan, where he was killed by the Indians in 1851.

In 1843 Philippi's first experience in the Strait was just beginning. On May 18, 1843, Intendant Espiñeira issued orders for the expedition to Captain Williams. Williams was instructed to make observations on ports, channels, tides, etc. on the trip to the Strait. Upon arrival he was to form an opinion about establishing steam tugs in the Strait and to pick the site for a fort, build it, name it Bulnes after the President of Chile, and turn it over to Lieutenant González Hidalgo. He was also ordered to conserve

80

supplies, help Philippi make observations of flora and fauna, maintain order, and comply with instructions. Included were additional instructions to maintain a fair distribution of food so there would be no shortage in case of an emergency, to investigate the possibilities for commercial lobster fishing after the fort and houses were completed, and to keep a diary.

The Ancud was ordered to leave the Strait for San Carlos with the crew and Philippi on September 1 or any convenient day near that date. George Mabon was given orders to remain at the fort to continue weather observations. If for some unavoidable reason the departure instructions could not be followed, the party was to wait for the arrival of the schooner Janequeo to bring supplies and reinforcements. If the Janequeo had not arrived by January 1, 1844, the entire party was to sail back to San Carlos. A document stating that Chile was not abandoning the fort but would return was to be buried at the foot of the flagpole in the fort. The Chilean flag was to be left flying. In an appendix, which Espiñeira added the following day, Williams was ordered to protest peacefully three times if a foreign nation were already established in the Strait. No force was to be used even if the foreign party were smaller. The same procedure was to be used if a foreign country occupied territory in the Strait after the arrival of the Chilean force.

The Ancud was scheduled to sail May 21, but her departure was delayed by unfavorable winds for one day. On the 26th the Ancud met a launch from Curaco with Charles Miller aboard. Miller, a lobster fisherman acquainted with the Strait and surrounding area, was persuaded to join the expedition. [8]

Unfavorable weather hit the Ancud, delaying her arrival in Puerto Americano until June 6. Captain Williams decided to put in long enough to build a small boat for use in exploring channels and tides and to repair storm damage. Within a month the repairs were completed, and the ship sailed south again. However, by August 4 the ship was back in Puerto Americano to repair severe damage caused by a storm a week earlier. This time, Captain Williams found it necessary to send Philippi with five men in the small boat back to Chiloé to get materials for the repairs. It was August 26 before Philippi returned with additional supplies and the items for the repairs.

While the Ancud was at Puerto Americano in June, she met the North American brigantine Enterprise under the command of Captain Benjamin Ash. Besides lobster fishing in what Chile regarded as her territorial waters, the Enterprise was engaged in illegal tobacco trade. When Williams returned to Puerto Americano in August, he found the North American ship still there and ordered Captain Ash to leave Chilean waters

81

by 10:00 A. M. September 5. The Enterprise did not leave, and Captain Williams warned Captain Ash that if he encountered the ship again he would report it to the government in Chiloé. Actually, the smaller Ancud could not do anything about the Enterprise, and Williams sailed away on the following day leaving the Enterprise undisturbed. The incident is significant only insofar as it indicates increased Chilean awareness of her sovereignty in this area.

A few days after leaving Puerto Americano, the Ancud entered Smyth Channel, and on September 17 her crew sighted Cape Tamar at the junction of Smyth Channel and the Strait. On September 18, Chilean Independence Day, the national flag flew for the first time in the waters of the Strait. A twenty-one gun salute was fired in honor of the occasion. Cape Forward in the center of the Strait was reached the next day, and two days after entering the Strait, the Ancud completed her outward voyage at Point Santa Ana, the site of Rey don Felipe or Port Famine.

Captain Williams' first act upon landing was to check the documents left by Captain Peacock when the Chile and the Peru sailed through the Strait in 1840 to see that they made no claim to the area. The documents were found to be inoffensive and permitted to remain, but the British money with the head of Queen Victoria was replaced with Chilean money bearing the national coat of arms. As soon as this task was completed, the whole company was brought ashore and assembled before the flagstaff while the Chilean flag was raised and honored with a twenty-one gun salute from the ship. At this time formal possession of the area was recorded, and a copy of the document, signed by all present including the women, was buried at the base of the flagpole. Another copy was retained by Captain Williams.

The next day, September 22, the French steam frigate Phaeton under the command of Louis Maissan anchored at Port Famine. The Phaeton was bound for the Marquesas Islands, which the French had recently claimed. Aboard were a bishop and his party of missionaries traveling to the new French possession. The following day another French ship, the brigantine Fleuris commanded by Captain Flathaway and bound from Africa to Chiloé, anchored in the bay. On Sunday, September 24, the French bishop and his party landed to say Mass in a tent from which the French flag flew, and on Monday French sailors went ashore with their flag to cut wood. Captain Williams formally protested to Lieutenant Maissan, who gave orders not to fly the French flag ashore. Lieutenant Maissan explained that the Strait had been considered unclaimed land and all vessels had formerly displayed their flags ashore. The French officer assured the Chileans that there had been no attempt to disregard the rights of Chile, but he told them that the final decision on the validity of the Chilean claim to the Strait would have to be made by the French government. This jurisdictional dispute did not disturb friendly relations between the two groups, for the Phaeton when she sailed carried the Chilean correspondence to Valparaiso.

After the departure of the French ships, the Ancud sailed on to the Atlantic Ocean, exploring the eastern half of the Strait and looking for a site on which to build the proposed fort. Returning to Point Santa Ana, the ship stopped on October 10, 1843, to place a tablet, one side of which bore the words República de Chile and the other side Viva Chile, in a prominent spot on Elizabeth Island. Captain Williams decided that Port Famine was the best site for the fort, and construction started immediately after his return on October 12.

Unfavorable weather delayed the work, but on October 30 the christening of the partially completed fort took place. The crew of the Ancud assembled ashore along with part of the crew from the North American brigantine Sapwing, owned and commanded by Captain Cristobal Lozado. Captain Lozado was the representative of Intendant Espiñeira. As the cannons began a twenty-one gun salute, Captain Williams raised the Chilean flag, named the fort Fuerte Bulnes, and broke a bottle of Chilean wine on the wall. The salute was first returned by the Sapwing and then by the Ancud. Finally, everyone was issued two rations of wine, and the rest of the night was spent celebrating.

By November 11 the fort was completed and supplied with food and ammunition. Lieutenant Manuel González Hidalgo received command of the fort and the troops as directed by Intendant Espiñeira's instructions, and George Mabon landed with his instruments for the observations which he had been instructed to continue after the departure of the Ancud. Before leaving for Chiloé, Captain Williams took three days to investigate the coal resources at Punta Arenas, Rocky Point, and Fresh Water Bay. He then returned to Fuerte Bulnes to give final instructions to Lieutenant González and to pick up the correspondence. On November 15 the Ancud sailed for Chiloé.

By the end of the month Williams had sailed out of the channels into the Gulf of Penas, where he met a small boat. Upon investigating, Captain Williams discovered that the French ship Fleuris had been shipwrecked by a storm before it left the Strait. Captain Williams took the occupants of the first boat aboard the Ancud and after overtaking the two remaining boats gave them a tow. Because of the extra load and unfavorable winds, the Ancud did not reach San Carlos until December 5. As soon as the ship was docked, the crew of the Ancud and the citizens of San Carlos began a wild celebration of the completion of the voyage.

Unlike Rey don Felipe, the colony founded by Sarmiento, Fuerte Bulnes was not forgotten by the government. In a decree dated January 3, 1844, Intendant Espiñeira named Sergeant Major Pedro Silva governor of the settlement in the Strait. Santiago Dunn, who knew English and French, accompanied Governor Silva as his secretary. Father Domingo Pasalini resigned as Guardian of the College of Jesus in Castro to become chaplain at Fuerte Bulnes. These officials traveled to Fuerte Bulnes on board the schooner Voladora, which sailed from San Carlos on January 20, 1844, with supplies and livestock for the new colony. Upon arriving at Fuerte Bulnes on February 8, Governor Silva received command of the fort from Lieutenant González Hidalgo. Governor Silva, a patriot officer of the Revolution, believed in rigid discipline. He commanded respect through terror, and his subordinates gave him the nickname Caliph.

The governor's unreasonable treatment of those under him earned him a great deal of ill-will during the short time he commanded Fuerte Bulnes. He followed Intendant Espiñeira's instructions to conserve food supplies to the point of declaring each member of the garrison eligible for only one ration regardless of marital status. After a short while the married couples began to show signs of their reduced diet. He used all of the available buildings to house the garrison and ordered the rest of the colony housed in one room. At the same time, he ordered the construction of a house for himself.

Fortunately, the Indians of the area were friendly. During the second visit of the Tehuelche Tribe, Governor Silva and Chief Santos Centurion signed a Treaty of Friendship and Commerce dated March 20, 1843. [9] The terms of the treaty provided for Indian recognition of Chilean sovereignty, regulation of trade between the two parties, and cooperation by both parties in case of invasion. Chile was particularly anxious to obtain the Indians' recognition of her sovereignty because the government of Argentina was attempting to achieve the same end.

Governor Silva temporarily relinquished his command of the colony on June 20, 1844. On that date the ketch Magallanes anchored with the new governor, José Justo de la Rivera, aboard. Under Justo de la Rivera, who was one of the revolutionists defeated at the Battle of Lircay in 1830, conditions in the colony did not greatly improve. Soldiers and colonists suffered severely from the cold during the winter months. Their suffering was aggravated by the fact that there was no clothing to replace that worn out by the soldiers working on the governor's house and the chapel that Justo de la Rivera ordered built. Near the end of 1845 Governor Justo de la Rivera was replaced by former Governor Pedro Silva. At the same time the old garrison was replaced by new troops from Chile. Earlier in the year, the Ancud had been permanently stationed at Fuerte Bulnes. The ship was used for exploring the area and maintaining law and order. There had been some smuggling in the Strait and around Chiloe.

By the time Silva returned to Fuerte Bulnes, the country's original enthusiasm for the colony had changed to disillusionment. There was even some debate about the practicality of continuing the colony because of the financial burden upon the government. Governor Silva began to consider the advisability of moving the colony from Point Santa Ana to a more hospitable location. Williams and Philippi had originally chosen this site because it possessed water and wood. Experience proved that other factors were more important than these initial considerations. If the colony were to prosper, it had to be able to produce a large part of its own food supply. The colonists found that the nature of the soil and the climate, especially the constant winds, at Fuerte Bulnes prevented the maturing of crops. Domestic animals brought from Chiloe failed to reproduce. The colony remained almost totally dependent on the government for subsistence.

No action was taken to move the colony until nearly a year after the arrival of a new governor, José de los Santos Mardones, in April of 1847. The new governor, a member of one of the oldest families in Santiago, was an army officer who had seen service in the independence movement. His military career had ended when his side lost the Battle of Lircay, but his appointment as Governor of the Strait colony had brought about his reinstatement in the army and his promotion to lieutenant colonel. In the fall of 1848 (March), a fire of undetermined origin destroyed more than half of the buildings at Fuerte Bulnes. Governor Santos Mardones decided to use this opportunity to move the colony to a more favorable location. The new site chosen by the governor was Punta Arenas on the Rio de Carbon. Although Punta Arenas is only fifty kilometers farther northeast in the Strait than Point Santa Ana, it has a more favorable climate and more fertile soil. The winds are not as constant as on Point Santa Ana.

Santos Mardones considered the new site necessary for the survival of the colony; so he proceeded with his plans without the permission of the Chilean government. He ordered the construction of accommodations for five hundred people at Punta Arenas, and in the fall of 1849 he transferred the population of Fuerte Bulnes to the new location. The governor then petitioned his new superior, the Minister of State in the Department of Marine, for permission to move the colony. Faced by a fait accompli, the government gave its permission. A law passed on August 30, 1848, had placed the Maritime Government of Magellan, comprising all the area south of Tres Montes Peninsula, under the direction of the Minister of State in the Department of Marine.[10]

Although Fuerte Bulnes was not completely abandoned, Punta Arenas became the colony in the Strait and has remained the center of population to the present day. The only inhabitants left in Fuerte Bulnes were some criminals transported from Chile. According to Governor Mardones' description of the colony in 1849, Punta Arenas consisted of thirty-one buildings in which one hundred thirty-nine individuals lived in comparative comfort. The new location proved beneficial for the colony, and it grew and became more prosperous.

The colony continued its peaceful existence until the Revolt of 1851. At the time of the revolt Benjamín Muñoz Gamero, the naval officer who had commanded the Magallanes during a voyage to the Strait in 1844, was governor. On the night of November 17 Lieutenant Miguel José Cambiaso led the convicts and prisoners in a successful attack upon the fort. When the fort fell Governor Muñoz, the priest, a few soldiers, and one wife escaped to the woods. They tried to reach a North American bark, the Florida, which was anchored off Punta Arenas, but their small boat was blown across the Strait to Tierra del Fuego.[11] The boat was prevented from landing there by a group of Indians who wounded one soldier with an arrow. The fugitives then went to Fuerte Bulnes where they hid, living on wild fruits and berries. Hunger caused one of the group to turn traitor and disclose the hiding place to the rebels. Cambiaso captured all of the escapees except two soldiers, who made their way to the western coast of the Strait where they found a Chilean ship, the Tres Amigos. The captives were taken back to Punta Arenas, and the governor and the priest were executed on December 3. Among the other victims of the revolt were three foreigners: Mr. Shaw, the owner of the Florida; Captain Talbot, commander of the Elisa Cornish; and a boy, the young son of the owner of the Elisa Cornish. The Elisa Cornish was bound from San Francisco to Liverpool with 90,000 to 100,000 pesos in gold and silver bullion and Mexican currency. The capture of this vessel gave the insurgents all the funds they needed.

As soon as the news of the revolt was received from the Tres Amigos, the government sent a military force to the Strait. When the soldiers arrived on December 4, they found the town deserted and all the buildings at least partially destroyed. Not until it became known that Cambiaso had left on the captured bullion ship, the Elisa Cornish, did the people begin to emerge from their hiding places in the woods. Cambiaso's attempt to escape to Europe was prevented by severe storms which drove him back through the Strait, finally sinking his ship in the Reina Adelade Archipelago. Soon after losing his ship, Cambiaso was captured. He was court-martialed and eventually executed.

It was after the Revolt of 1851 that Bernardo Philippi was named governor and entrusted with the task of re-establishing the colony in the Strait. Shortly after his arrival at Punta Arenas, Governor Philippi made a trip into the interior to visit the Indians. He made the journey with only his assistant and an interpreter. On October 27 the Indians assassinated the governor and his assistant and took the interpreter prisoner. The interpreter later escaped and returned to the colony with the story of the assassination. One explanation is that the Indians were retaliating for the treatment they had received from Cambiaso during the revolt. Another is that the Indians who killed the governor simply wanted his horses and clothing.

In 1877 another uprising similar to the one in 1851 took place. Convicts and soldiers seized control of the settlement while the gunboat was away surveying a distant area of the Strait. Again a large part of the buildings were burned, and all the stores and houses were looted. Several colonists were killed by the soldiers during their drunken brawls. This undisciplined mob was easily driven into the interior when the governor, who had managed to escape in a small boat, returned with the Chilean gunboat Magallanes. Most of the mutineers were either the victims of starvation or their own disputes, and the rest were captured and jailed by Argentina as they tried to escape through Argentine territory.

In spite of these internal difficulties, Punta Arenas continued to grow. This growth continued even after the opening of the Panama Canal in 1914 greatly decreased the importance of the city in world shipping, and by 1972 the settlement had a population of approximately 50,000. Punta Arenas is the only city that has ever prospered in the Strait. Its early success was based upon its location as a port of call for world shipping. The coal deposits in the area gave the colony additional value as a refueling station for steamships on the long voyage around the continent. The settlement was also the center of trade with the Indians of Patagonia and Tierra del Fuego. About the time the Panama Canal supplanted the Strait as a major shipping route, the sheep industry began to flourish in the area around the city, and Punta Arenas became the center of trade in wool and hides. After 1950 the development of the oil fields discovered in 1945 on Tierra del Fuego and in the eastern end of the Strait of Magellan broadened the economic basis of the region and made it somewhat more important to the Chilean economy.

Economic development in the area was not the only or even the most important reason for Chile's original interest in establishing the colony. One of the main objectives in founding the colony in the Strait was to make effective her claim to the area. In this objective Chile was successful. Neither France nor England made any further gestures toward the Strait. Only Argentina protested the Chilean activity in the Strait, and after years of intermittent negotiations between the two countries, the Chilean claim was admitted.

NOTES

1. Philip Parker King, Robert Fitz Roy, Charles Darwin, Narrative of the Surveying Voyages of His Majesty's Ships Adventure and Beagle, between the years 1826 and 1836, describing their Examination of the Southern Shores of South America, and the Beagle's Circumnavigation of the Globe, 3 vols. (London: Henry Colburn, 1839).
2. King, Narrative, 1, pp. 152-153.
3. Anguita, Leyes, p. 252.
4. Armando Braun Menéndez, Fuerte Bulnes: Historia de la ocupación del Estrecho de Magallanes por el Gobierno de Chile en 1843, precedida de una Crónica somera de aquel paso de mar y los antecedentes de la expedición; viaje de la goleta "Ancud", fundación del Fuerte Bulnes y secesos ocurridos hasta el translado de la colonia a Punta Arenas en 1849 (Buenos Aires: Emecé Editores, 1943), p. 54.
5. Jorge Mabon, "Informe al Ministro de Estado en el Departamento de Interior y de Relaciones Exteriores," dated April 19, 1844, published in El Araucano, Santiago, Chile, April 26, 1844.
6. Nicolás Anrique R., ed., Diario de la Goleta Ancud al mando del Capitán de Fragata don Juan Guillermos (1843) Para tomar posesión del Estrecho de Magallanes (Santiago: Emprenta, Litografia i Encuadernación Barcelona, 1901).
7. R. A. Philippi, "Apuntes Biograficos sobre mi hermano Bernardo Philippi," published in Anrique R., Diario, pp. 115-123.
8. Carlos•E. Miller, Viaje de la goleta de guerra "Ancud" para tomar posesión del Estrecho de Magallanes. El práctico d. Carlos Miller (Ancud, Chile: 1901).
9. Braun Menéndez, Fuerte Bulnes, pp. 225-226.
10. Anguita, Leyes, p. 503.
11. For an eyewitness account by the Captain of the Florida see Charles

H. Brown, *Insurrection at Magellan: Narrative of the Imprisonment and Escape of Capt. Chas. H. Brown, from the Chilean Convicts* (Boston: Geo. C. Rand, 1854).

CHAPTER 7. THE ANDES BOUNDARY

CHILEAN expansion to the south led to a dispute with Argentina over Patagonia and the Strait of Magellan. When Chile founded Fuerte Bulnes on Brunswick Peninsula in 1842, she occupied territory that Argentina claimed. Because the news of Chile's colony in the Strait did not reach Buenos Aires for about two years, Argentina did not immediately press her claim to the southern portion of the continent. It was not until December of 1847 that Argentina formally protested the invasion of her territory.[1]

In the note of protest, the Argentine government stated that the eastern summit of the Andes as far as Cape Horn marked the western limit of Argentine sovereignty. Fuerte Bulnes, situated east of this line, was without question in Argentine territory. Furthermore, Patagonia had been placed under the jurisdiction of Buenos Aires by the Spanish crown when the Viceroyalty of Río de la Plata was created in 1776; therefore, according to the doctrine of the uti posidetis of 1810, it constituted a portion of the Argentine Republic. The note concluded by stating that the Argentine minister in Chile would be provided with the additional documents necessary to resolve the matter if Chile deemed this statement insufficient.

The following year the two governments exchanged notes concerning the ownership of Patagonia, the Strait, and a few valleys in the Andes called potreros. In a note dated August 30, 1848, the Chilean minister suggested that the two governments exchange proof of their titles and appoint a joint commission to mark the boundary on the ground in accordance with the documents. As soon as the marking was completed the boundary line would be subject to ratification by both nations.

Argentina replied in November that each nation should make known to the other its titles to the disputed territory in order to arrive at a fair and equitable solution in conformity with the rights of both. The note stated that Argentina had always considered her rights to the territory in question clear and sufficient. Although she recognized the advisability of marking the boundary, she held that this procedure was possible only after an ex-

90

change of titles had resulted in agreement. Argentina pointed out that she was not able to participate in immediate boundary discussions because of internal problems and the Anglo-French intervention. The problems referred to in the note resulted for the most part from the desire of Juan Manuel de Rosas, the ruler of Argentina, to incorporate Uruguay into the Argentine Confederation. He gave aid and encouragement to pro-Argentine gauchos in Uruguay and attempted for nine years to blockade Montevideo. The attempted blockade of Montevideo eventually involved England and France, who cooperated in a blockade of Buenos Aires from 1845 to 1848.

Even without Argentina's preoccupation with her other problems, the note continued, preparations for the boundary discussions would be a time-consuming task. All of the necessary documents would have to be collected and prepared. Argentina stated that although she could not give the problem her immediate attention, she was willing to discuss the boundary question at the earliest possible time and would send a minister with full instructions at some later date. Consequently, boundary discussions were deferred indefinitely by Argentina.

The disputed potreros are located between the two ranges of the Andes separating Chile from the Argentine province of Mendoza. The eastern range is higher, but the western range is the water divide. Chilean access to the valleys is easier because of the lower passes and less rugged mountains. The valleys were used by Chileans for summer pastures, hence the name potreros. In some valleys Chileans paid a grazing fee to the province of Mendoza.

The federal government of Argentina at first did not concern itself with the problem of these valleys, but the governors of Mendoza did. In 1846 Governor Celendonio de la Cuesta appointed a two-man commission to survey the valleys and river courses. The commission reported a year later the valleys must be considered Argentine territory because the rivers in these valleys are tributaries of Argentine rivers. The commission also cited the fees collected by the province of Mendoza as proof of the Argentine claim, but the main principle advanced for demarcation was the divortia aquarum. The fact that access from Argentina was so difficult that Argentine use was impractical was not considered. During later discussions Argentina refused to recognize either the divortia aquarum or continued use of a disputed area as proof of a claim.

The Argentine minister mentioned in the note of 1848 arrived in Chile in 1855, seven years after the announcement of the mission. During those years Argentina was preoccupied with internal problems. In February, 1852, President Rosas was overthrown by General Justo José de Ur-

quiza, caudillo of Entre Rios. Urquiza, leader of the federalist forces of
the interior, obtained control of all of Argentina except the province of
Buenos Aires, which continued its intermittent warfare with the Argentine
Confederation. A new constitution was written at the Congress of Tucuman
in 1853 and accepted by all the provinces except Buenos Aires. Although
Buenos Aires did not join the Argentine Confederation, she did end her warfare with it, and General Urquiza was able to turn his attention to foreign
affairs. An agreement with Chile in 1855 provided for the construction of
the Transandean Railroad, but no boundary accord was reached. Instead,
the two nations concluded a treaty of friendship, commerce, and navigation, which was ratified the following year. Only one clause, article
thirty-four, referred to the boundaries. It read:

> Both contracting parties recognize as the boundaries of their re-
> spective territories, those which they possessed at the time of
> their separation from Spanish rule in 1810, and agree to postpone
> the questions which have arisen, or may arise, on this matter, to
> discuss them afterwards in a friendly manner without ever re-
> sorting to violent measures, and in case of not reaching complete
> agreement, to submit the decision to the arbitration of a friendly
> nation. [2]

In this clause both nations recognize the doctrine of the <u>uti posidetis</u> of
1810 as the basis for determining the boundary and pledge a peaceful settlement. They also agree to arbitrate if necessary. However, no attempt
to reach an accord was made at that time and the dispute continued.

It should be noted that to this date Argentina had never made any
attempt to exercise sovereignty in Patagonia or Tierra del Fuego in support of her claim. Argentina had no colony in the area nor any administrative organization for the area. Chile, on the other hand, had established
a colony at Punta Arenas, stationed administrative officials in the Strait,
and assigned supervisory responsibility to a cabinet level officer in Santiago.

The continuing civil conflict in Argentina erupted in a new period of
open warfare, and between 1859 and 1861 the struggle between Bartolome
Mitre, the leader of Buenos Aires, and General Urquiza prevented Argentina from taking up the boundary question. When discussions were finally
resumed, Chile took the initial step. Her minister in Argentina, Jose Victoria Lastorria, offered a compromise settlement which would have given
Chile Tierra del Fuego and southern Patagonia. Chile would have received
the territory lying west and south of a line running from Gregorio Bay, located approximately one quarter of the way through the Strait from the At-

lantic, northward to 50° latitude and then along the eastern range of the Andes to Reloncavi Inlet, across the Gulf of Ancud from Chiloé. Argentina would have received northern Patagonia and the Atlantic coast to the Strait. The northern side of the entrance to the Strait would have been Argentine and the southern side Chilean. Argentina refused to accept the compromise because she would not recognize any Chilean claim to Patagonia and she did not want any part of the Atlantic entrance to the Strait in the possession of Chile.

The boundary discussion proposed in the first exchange of notes in 1848 did not occur until 1872, six years after the failure of the Lastorria compromise. During this period both nations fought a war. Argentina, allied with Brazil and Uruguay, fought the Paraguayan War between 1865 and 1871, and Chile joined the other Pacific coast nations in a war against Spain from 1865 to 1870. Following these wars Félix Frías became Argentine minister in Chile, and he opened negotiations. Argentina offered a compromise line running from Peckett Bay in the Strait westward to the Cordillera of the Andes. Argentina would obtain Patagonia and the eastern portion of the Strait; Chile would receive only the western part of the Strait, which included Brunswick Peninsula on which Punta Arenas is located. Chile rejected the proposed line, which gave Argentina almost all the territory in dispute. Chilean Foreign Minister Adolfo Ibañez offered as a counterproposal the forty-fifth parallel from the Atlantic to the Pacific Ocean, from Cabo Dos Bahias on the Atlantic to Isla Magdalena in the Pacific. The Chilean counterproposal would have more equally divided the disputed territory by giving Argentina northern Patagonia and Chile southern Patagonia and the Strait.

Argentina not only rejected the Ibañez proposal but also began to expand her effective control into the area. In 1873 President Domingo Sarmiento sent to the Argentine congress the draft of a law for organizing the territory of Patagonia and determining the boundaries. The law passed by congress organized the territory and established procedures for colonization. Chile immediately protested the Argentine attempt to exercise sovereignty in the disputed area. When she acknowledged receipt of the note of protest, Argentina explained that no change had occurred as a result of the law. At this point Chile decided that no boundary line could be agreed upon and terminated negotiations by instructing her minister in Buenos Aires, Guillermo Blest Gana, to request the arbitration provided for in the Treaty of 1856. At the end of April, 1874, Argentine Minister of Foreign Affairs Carlos Tejador accepted arbitration as the means to solve the boundary problem.

Although both nations formally accepted arbitration, no arbitration protocol could be concluded. Chile accused President Nicolás Avellaneda of opposing arbitration and delaying negotiations. As proof of her charge she cited the speech of Foreign Minister Bernardo de Irigoyen to congress in 1881. Irigoyen said:

> The President of the Republic undertook to consider that complicated question of the boundary, and the first resolution was to maintain integrally the jurisdiction of the Republic all along the coast of the Atlantic, and to defend her rights to the vast stretch of Patagonia, endeavoring to guard it by all such means as prudence should suggest from the inconvenience and danger of arbitration to which it was already pledged. [3]

In the same speech Irigoyen added:

> We therefore had to accept the facts as we found them, and to manoeuvre, if I may use this word, in the most convenient manner to attain our objective; the constant idea which as Minister of Foreign Affairs I have held in this matter: to save Patagonia from the risks of an arbitral decision. [4]

In countercharges Argentina placed the responsibility for delay on Foreign Minister Ibañez, citing his note of July 31, 1875, in which he stated that it was impossible to reach an agreement or to name an arbitrator. [5] Chile responded that the Ibañez note expressed a statement of fact, not official policy. She cited her note of August 22, 1874, in which she formally accepted arbitration, and noted that she had consented to delay an arbitration agreement only until President Avellaneda took office in 1874.

Progress seemed possible in 1876. Chile appointed as her representative in Buenos Aires Diego Barros Arana, one of her most famous historians and educators. In July Barros Arana and Irigoyen began discussions to conclude either a boundary agreement or an arbitration protocol. Argentina submitted a proposal that drew a line from Mount Dinero northward to 52° 19', thence west and north along the elevation of hills to Mount Aymond at 52° 10', and along this line to the Cordillera of the Andes. Tierra del Fuego was divided by the latitude line at 68° 34' passing through Cape Espíritu Santo to the Beagle Channel. Argentina would receive the islands east and north, the largest being Staten Island, and Chile would receive those west and south including Cape Horn. The Chilean government could not accept these terms and again requested arbitration.

Further negotiations between Barros Arana and Irigoyen resulted in a six point agreement as the basis for arbitration. This agreement was completed in January, 1877. The first five points dealt with the selection of an arbitrator and procedural matters. Point six set forth a general demarcation principle for the Andes boundary: "From 50° northward the boundary of both countries shall be the summit of the Cordillera of the Andes whether the most culminating points are selected, or the water parting line."[6] Foreign Minister Ibañez rejected this general demarcation principle because it would have required Chile to relinquish her claim to Patagonia.

Negotiations were resumed in April and extended into May. Another agreement had been reached when Barros Arana received instructions to insist upon the divortia aquarum as the demarcation principle for that portion of the Andes not in dispute. In other words Chile would accept the water divide as the demarcation principle for the northern Andes but would not limit the boundary to the Andes in Patagonia. Earlier Chilean proposals demonstrate Chile's insistence upon exerting her claim to Patagonia. Some of these proposals would have given Chile an Atlantic coast. Barros Arana had already signed a new arbitration agreement when his new instructions arrived. The Chilean government officially rejected this agreement on the grounds that one clause permitted both nations to exercise jurisdiction in Patagonia during arbitration. A more plausible explanation is the failure of the agreement to incorporate Chile's new terms.

Article one of the 1877 agreement rejected by Chile was a compromise of the demarcation principles advanced by both nations. Although the 1877 document was rejected, the demarcation compromise it contained remained viable. This basic compromise appeared again in the proposed arbitration agreement of 1878 and was ultimately part of the Boundary Treaty of 1881. "The Republic of Chile is divided from the Argentine Republic by the Cordillera of the Andes; the boundary line running through the highest points of this chain, passing between the sources which flow down the two slopes."[7] The 1878 proposal was the 1877 agreement with one article added to provide for the determination of the boundary where the water divide is not clear. Chile found this agreement no more acceptable than the one of the previous year.

From 1876 to 1879 Chile and Argentina tried unsuccessfully to draft a boundary treaty or an arbitration agreement. Beginning in 1878 public opinion in both countries became inflamed and created obstacles for a peaceful solution.[8] The outbreak of the War of the Pacific in 1879 exacerbated the already increasing feeling of hostility between the two countries. Chile was afraid that Argentina would join the secret alliance which Peru and Bolivia had concluded against her, but a boundary dispute with Bolivia caused Argentina to be cautious. Argentine interest in foreign affairs was distracted for a while when civil strife between the province of Buenos Aires and the federal government erupted in June, 1880, after the defeat of the Buenos Aires presidential candidate, Carlos Tejedor. Newly elected President Julio Roca federalized the capital city following a brief, unsuccessful military campaign waged by the province and city of Buenos Aires against the federal government. Preoccupation with her internal problems brought about a temporary abatement of Argentina's growing hostility toward Chile, but Chile became more anti-Argentine even though she was devoting most of her attention to the War of the Pacific. Relations between the two nations were never formally broken although neither government had a representative in the capital of the other.

Chile experienced little difficulty in defeating Peru and Bolivia and had captured Lima, virtually ending the war, when the ministers of the United States in Chile and Argentina in April, 1881, offered their friendly services in reopening negotiations. Since neither nation any longer found its domestic or foreign problems pressing, the offer was accepted, and Thomas A. Osborn in Santiago and Thomas O. Osborn in Buenos Aires began talks. [9] They decided to use as a starting point the correspondence of two prominent Argentine citizens, Luis Sáenz Peña, later president of Argentina, and Mariano de Sarratea, then residing in Chile. The two gentlemen had been corresponding about the boundary problem. Each had drawn up a set of terms acceptable to the government of the republic in which he was residing.

Sarratea in May telegraphed the Chilean terms to his colleague. Chile favored limited arbitration and a compromise based upon the Barros Arana-Irigoyen agreement of 1876. The division of Tierra del Fuego at the latitude of Cape Espíritu Santo would be retained, but the line in Patagonia would be submitted to arbitration. The Patagonian line to be arbitrated ran from Possession Bay on the north side of the Strait, just inside the eastern end, northwesterly to 52° in the Andes. The cordillera would be the boundary north of the fifty-second parallel, and the Strait would be free.

The Chilean terms, Sáenz Peña felt, would be acceptable to Argentina provided an adequate explanation of those terms could be reached. The explanation would have to include neutralization of the Strait with a pledge by each nation not to fortify the area. That part of the Strait from Mount Dinero to Point Delgada, a line approximately fifty miles farther west than that proposed by Chile, should be submitted to arbitration as well as the remaining boundary line in Patagonia up to 52°. Tierra del Fuego could be divided as it had been in the 1876 accord.

When Thomas A. Osborn conferred with Chilean officials in the first week in May, he was given another basis for settlement. The line would be drawn from the watershed at 52° to the meridian 70° longitude and thence southward to Cape Virgines. The area south of the line would be Chilean except Staten Island and the area north would be Argentine. This settlement would be definitive. In the event either side demanded arbitration, a single arbitrator would decide who should exercise sovereignty over the territory in question. If the arbitrator decided that Chile had gained Argentine territory, he would also decide the monetary compensation Chile would pay; no territory would be exchanged. The Strait would be neutralized, and each nation would agree not to erect fortifications on its shores. Under this proposal Chile would have received all of Tierra del Fuego and the Strait, and Argentina would have received Staten Island and northern Patagonia. The line proposed for Patagonia is approximately the one which later became the boundary.

On May 11 Thomas O. Osborn in Buenos Aires replied with a counterproposal from the Argentine government. The first part of the compromise remained the same. Staten Island would be Argentine and the Strait would be neutralized. The rest of the newest Chilean proposal was unacceptable. Argentina wanted Tierra del Fuego divided by the 1876 line. She offered a new line for Patagonia. The new boundary would begin at the watershed on the fifty-second parallel and run in a straight line to Point Dungeness.

A week later Mr. Osborn in Santiago answered that the accuracy of the previous telegram was questioned by Chilean officials. The proposed line running from the water divide at 52° straight to Point Dungeness would in places cross water; the line was to be a land boundary. Chile also felt that all of Tierra del Fuego should belong to her in order to prevent confusion. Argentina could be compensated for the loss of Tierra del Fuego with territory on the north coast of the Strait in the vicinity of Point Dungeness.

The United States minister in Buenos Aires replied on May 20 that Argentina insisted upon the partition of Tierra del Fuego as earlier agreed upon. He explained that if the line proposed by Argentina extending from 52° to Point Dungeness crossed water, it would do so at Watering Place on Possession Bay. The area south of the line between Watering Place and Point Dungeness would be Chilean. If the line ran overland, all of the shore of Possession Bay would be Chilean. The two nations were not too far apart. The various lines drawn in Patagonia from 52° to the Atlantic entrance to the Strait were not widely separated. There was still disagreement over whether or not Tierra del Fuego should be divided, but Chile had earlier accepted the concept of division. Another difference was over the question of arbitration. Chile wanted a direct settlement with compensation for Argentina, and Argentina preferred arbitration.

The next day Mr. Osborn in Santiago telegraphed an explanation of the Chilean proposal. The line north of 52º as well as south would be established by direct negotiations, and arbitration would be limited to the determination of monetary compensation. A direct settlement was preferable in the view of Chile since major differences existed over an arbitration agreement. Argentina still considered the proposal unacceptable.

Following a further exchange of views, the Chilean Minister of Foreign Affairs, Melquiades Valderrama, submitted a new set of terms drawn from the ideas expressed by both governments. The first point established the Cordillera of the Andes as the boundary as far south as 52º latitude. "The boundary line shall run in that extent over the highest summits of the said Cordillera which divide the waters."[10] Also included was a provision for appointing two experts to settle differences arising in certain valleys formed by the bifurcation of the cordillera and in places where the water parting line was not clear.

The second clause drew the line from the Strait to 52º latitude. The boundary would start at Point Dungeness on the Strait and run by land to Mount Dinero from which point it would follow the highest elevation of the chain of hills stretching westward to Mount Aymond. From this point the line would continue to the intersection of the seventieth meridian with the fifty-second parallel, thence westward along the parallel to the water divide of the Andes. The third clause divided Tierra del Fuego in accordance with the 1876 agreement along the meridian 68º 34' from the Strait to the Beagle Channel. The area east of this line would be Argentine as well as the islands situated east and north, in other words, the islands in the Atlantic. The land west of the meridian would be Chilean as well as the islands south and west including Cape Horn.

The fourth provision of the proposed agreement stated that the experts referred to in the first article would mark the boundary, including that part of it established by the preceding two bases, using the procedure provided in article one. Section five neutralized the Strait and assured free navigation to all nations. The last section provided for arbitration in case of any dispute arising from the agreement. The two governments were given perpetual sovereignty over the territory granted to each by this agreement. Questions which might arise from the agreement or from other causes would be submitted to the arbitration of a friendly nation, but under no circumstances would the boundary established by the agreement be changed.

On June 4 Foreign Minister Irigoyen notified Mr. Osborn that his government would accept the six points with some modification of the first and fifth bases. The first section was reworded to read, "The boundary line shall run in that extent along the highest summits of the said Cordillera which divide the waters and shall pass between the streams (vertientes) flowing down to either side."[11] Irigoyen stated that this addition supplemented but did not change the first clause. Chile accepted the reworded clause.

The fifth section was changed by Argentina to prohibit explicitly the construction of any fortifications on the coasts of the Strait of Magellan. Chile found the change unacceptable. She was willing to neutralize the Strait and to grant free navigation, but she was not willing to limit her sovereignty in the Strait by accepting a prohibition against fortifications which would not impede free navigation. An additional exchange of views between the two capitals resulted in the formulation of a new statement by Foreign Minister Valderrama in Santiago. "The Straits of Magellan shall be neutralized forever, and free navigation assured to the flags of all nations. In order to assure this freedom and neutrality, no fortification or military defense shall be constructed on the coast that might be contrary to this purpose."[12]

The next day, June 26, Argentina approved the change. The six articles became the Boundary Treaty of 1881, which was signed in Buenos Aires on July 23 by Consul General Francisco B. de Echeverria for Chile and by Foreign Minister Bernardo de Irigoyen for Argentina.[13] The treaty was ratified and exchanged on October 22 in Santiago. The two nations looked forward to a friendly and rapid demarcation of the boundary in accordance with the provisions of the treaty.

NOTES

1. The documents concerned with the early period of dispute are printed in Appendix to the Statement Presented on Behalf of Chile in Reply to the Argentine Report submitted to the Tribunal Constituted by H. B. Majesty's Government acting as Arbitrator in pursuant of the Agreement dated April 17, 1896, 2 vols. (London: Butler & Tanner, 1902).

2. Statement Presented on Behalf of Chile in Reply to the Argentine Re-

port submitted to the Tribunal Constituted by H. B. Majesty's Government acting as Arbitrator in pursuant of the Agreement dated April 17, 1896, 4 vols. (London: Butler & Tanner, 1901-1902), 1, p. 202.

3. Statement Presented on Behalf of Chile, 1, p. 211.
4. Statement Presented on Behalf of Chile, 1, p. 212.
5. Bernardo de Irigoyen, Question des Limites entre la République Argentine et le Chile (Buenos Aires: Imprenta Oswald y Martinez, 1881), p. 30.
6. Statement Presented on Behalf of Chile, 1, pp. 245-246.
7. Irigoyen, Question des Limites, pp. 33-34.
8. See the reports of United States ministers Thomas A. Osborn in Santiago and Thomas O. Osborn in Buenos Aires in Papers Relating to the Foreign Relations of the United States, 1878, 1879, 1880, 1881.
9. Appendix to the Statement Presented on Behalf of Chile, 1, pp. 208-235.
10. Appendix to the Statement Presented on Behalf of Chile, 1, p. 219.
11. Appendix to the Statement Presented on Behalf of Chile, 1, p. 224.
12. Appendix to the Statement Presented on Behalf of Chile, 1, p. 235.
13. Bascuñan Montes, Recopilación, 2, pp. 120-125.

CHAPTER 8. DEMARCATION AND ARBITRATION

CHILE and Argentina began discussions to implement the Treaty of 1881 almost as soon as it was ratified. The discussions immediately disclosed major differences between the two nations on the interpretation of the demarcation principle in article one.

> The boundary between Chile and the Argentine Republic is from
> north to south, as far as the 52nd parallel of latitude, the Cordi-
> llera de los Andes. The boundary line shall run in that extent over
> the highest summits of the said Cordillera which divide the waters,
> and shall pass between the sources of streams flowing down to
> either side. The difficulties that might arise owing to the exist-
> ence of certain valleys formed by the bifurcation of the Cordillera,
> and where the water divide shall not be clear, shall be amicably
> solved by two Experts, appointed one by each party. Shall these
> fail to agree, a third Expert, selected by both Governments, will
> be called in to decide them. A Minute of their proceedings shall be
> drawn up in duplicate, signed by the Experts, and it shall be con-
> sidered stable and valid without the necessity of further formalities
> or proceedings. A copy of such Minute shall be forwarded to each
> of the Governments.[1]

Argentina considered the principle of demarcation a geographic one, the highest peaks of the Andes; Chile considered it a hydrographic one, the water-parting line. The western peaks of the Cordillera are the highest ones, but the water-parting line is in the eastern peaks. In places the wa-ter-parting line is considerably farther east than the highest peaks.

There were also difficulties in organizing the commission of experts charged in article one with the responsibility of marking the boundary. The appointment of the experts was delayed first by Chilean involvement in the War of the Pacific and later by a disagreement over the duties of the com-mission.[2] Argentina initiated discussions that resulted after two years in a protocol organizing the commission, but the protocol was not signed until August of 1888. In the protocol the two nations agreed to name experts within two months of its ratification and provided for the appointment of five assistants for each country. The number of assistants could be increased later upon request of the experts as long as each nation had an equal number. The assistants were authorized to mark the boundary, but the experts were charged with the task of drawing up written instructions to guide the work. Forty days after their appointment the experts were to meet in Concepción, Chile, to begin work. Should the experts be unable to agree, the governments of Chile and Argentina would appoint a third party to settle the differences. The nations would jointly share the costs of demarcation.

During the two years following the signing of the protocol, Chile and Argentina attempted to define the powers and procedures of the commission of experts and to begin the actual work of marking the boundary. These discussions delayed ratification of the protocol signed in 1888 until January, 1890. Argentina then appointed Octavio Pico as her expert, and Chile appointed Diego Barros Arana. The experts met in Concepción on the appointed day, April 20. In the first working session it became evident that the two experts had very different points of view. Nevertheless, after some discussion they were able to agree that they would start demarcation in Tierra del Fuego and at San Francisco Pass between the twenty-sixth and the twenty-seventh parallels. The pass was recognized as a point on the boundary and not as the northern point of the boundary. North of this point was the former Bolivian littoral over which the War of the Pacific had been fought. At this time Chile had control over the area under the 1884 Treaty of Truce, but she did not gain sovereignty until the peace treaty was signed in 1904. Without sovereignty she could not decide boundaries.

The basic disagreement over interpretation of the demarcation principle remained. Sr. Pico returned to Buenos Aires in June before the mountain passes became closed for the winter, and communication by mail was very slow. The Argentine expert maintained that he was willing to draft instructions on technical procedures, but he could not discuss the interpretation of article one of the boundary treaty because the experts were not authorized to do so. The treaty established the boundary; the experts only marked the boundary on the ground. Sr. Barros Arana, on the other hand, said that the instructions which the experts were required by the treaty to write had to be based upon an interpretation of article one. No agreement on instructions was possible without agreement on interpretation.

Several incidents delayed further meetings of the experts. A change
of government in Argentina postponed discussions from August to November
of 1890. Pico did not leave Buenos Aires until December. By that time the
Revolution of 1891 had broken out in Chile, and Sr. Barros Arana was re-
lieved of his duties as Chilean expert by President José Manuel Balmaceda
in January, 1891. During the revolution no work was attempted by the commission of experts. When the revolution was ended by the overthrow of
Balmaceda in August, Barros Arana was reappointed to his former post.
However, no meeting of the experts took place until January, 1892.

When meetings resumed in Santiago at the beginning of the new year,
Sr. Pico proposed four bases for the instructions to the assistants. First,
article one of the treaty should be applied strictly; second, when the highest
summits of the cordillera are tablelands or plateaus, the highest point
thereon should be determined by leveling and the dividing line run over
these points; third, even if the highest peaks are inaccessible they should
be the true boundary; and fourth, if in some valleys formed by the bifurcation of the cordillera the water-parting line is not clear, the joint commission should draw an exact map and submit it to the experts for a decision.
Sr. Pico also stated that the general rule of demarcation included in the
treaty was the highest summits of the Cordillera of the Andes.

Sr. Barros Arana replied that the boundary could not deviate from
the water-parting line even if the highest peaks were not situated thereon.
The geographic irregularities of the Andes made it impossible to draw a
boundary line over the highest peaks. Since article one of the treaty used
the terminology, "the highest summits of the cordillera which divide the
waters," Barros Arana concluded only those highest peaks which divide the
waters could be on the boundary line. The Argentine expert had no authority to continue the matter and referred the question to his government.

Argentina wanted demarcation to proceed in spite of the disagreement and in February persuaded Chile to agree. By the end of February
the two experts were able to give their assistants oral instructions for demarcation in Tierra del Fuego and in the northernmost section. Only those
points on which there was agreement would be marked. Misfortune struck
unexpectedly at the beginning of April; Sr. Pico died suddenly. To prevent
a delay President Carlos Pellegrini appointed a replacement, Valentin Virasoro, within a week. However, no significant progress could be made
until the new expert reached Santiago, and it was not until January, 1893,
that Virasoro arrived. Because of the approach of winter, it was imperative that work begin immediately if any demarcation were to be accomplished in 1893.

As agreed upon in 1890, demarcation began in Tierra del Fuego and in San Francisco Pass. No real problems were encountered in Tierra del Fuego because of the definite statement describing this boundary in the treaty. The marker in San Francisco Pass was a different matter. Even though the mixed commission did agree temporarily upon the site for a marker, it could not agree upon the reason for placing it there. The record of placing the marker in San Francisco Pass demonstrates the views held by the two nations.[3] The Chilean assistants drew up a draft of the record in which the water-parting line determined the site of the marker. The Argentine assistants explained the position of the marker on the basis of highest point. A compromise of the two statements could not be found, and both were forwarded to the experts. It was clearly evident that demarcation could not continue without agreement on the basic principle, but the experts ignored this fact and continued the attempt to solve their problems on a procedural basis in order to avoid breaking off all efforts to mark the boundary on the ground.

In March Sr. Virasoro and Sr. Barros Arana decided to prepare a written statement of the differences which prevented them from completing the instructions required by the Protocol of 1888. Before they could write it, the Argentine Minister in Chile and the Foreign Minister of Chile intervened. Together the four men arrived at an agreement which became the Protocol of May 1, 1893.

The new protocol was designed to eliminate all the differences that had developed since the boundary treaty had been ratified twelve years before. The principle of demarcation stated in article one of the new protocol was exactly the same as the one stated in article one of the boundary treaty and became the invariable rule to be followed in future proceedings. As a consequence all waters east of the cordillera were Argentine and those west Chilean. Clause two assured each nation sovereignty over its littoral. It expressly stated that Chile could not claim any points toward the Atlantic nor Argentina any toward the Pacific. Although Chile felt that the boundary treaty had already established this principle, she requested that a specific statement be included in the 1893 protocol to void claims being advanced by some Argentine citizens to Pacific waters and ports. The remaining clauses repeated provisions from earlier agreements providing for dates to begin boundary marking, mapping of valleys in doubt, and other technical arrangements. A third subcommission was set up to accelerate the pace of marking the boundary on the ground. The final provision, inserted by Chile, reaffirmed the validity of the Treaty of 1881 and insured that the demarcation principle would come before an arbitrator. Chile was convinced that no direct settlement could be reached and that arbitration, which she had been suggesting for twenty years, would be necessary.

As soon as the protocol was signed, Barros Arana presented Virasoro with a draft of the instructions required by the Treaty of 1881 and the Protocols of 1888 and 1893. The principle of demarcation was the water-parting line. Sr. Virasoro was returning to Buenos Aires and took the draft with him. Soon after returning home, he became Minister of Foreign Affairs and did not return to Santiago in October as he had planned. Norbert Quirno Costa, who as Argentine Minister in Santiago had helped negotiate the Protocol of 1893, became the Argentine expert. At the end of the year a modified draft of the Barros Arana instructions was delivered to Chile by the new expert. The most important change was in the principle of demarcation, which Argentina insisted was the peculiar water-parting line of the principal chain of the Cordillera of the Andes. Chile was totally unwilling to accept the change. Since both countries considered it desirable to continue marking the boundary in those areas where no differences existed, a compromise on the instructions was arranged. The compromise set of instructions consisted of restating article one of the boundary treaty. Consequently, the basic difference in interpretation of the demarcation principle was ignored once again, and true progress could not be made.

The failure is amply demonstrated by the renewed attempt to continue boundary marking. The first subcommission began work in the central portion of the Andes at Las Damas Pass. The same day they arrived, the commissioners were able to place a boundary marker. However, the writing of the record of their action presented the same problems as the record of the marker at San Francisco Pass. Sr. Alejandro Bertrand, the head of the Chilean members of the subcommission, insisted that the statement should cite the water-parting line as the basis for placing the marker. His Argentine counterpart, Luis F. Dellepiane, wanted to use the principal chain of the Andes instead. A combination of the two statements was finally used. Only one other marker was placed, the one in Santa Elena Pass thirty kilometers south, before Argentina requested a suspension of activity at the end of March. Winter set in before work was resumed. Other subcommissions sent out in 1894 to mark other sections of the boundary were no more successful. No marking occurred in 1895.

Throughout 1894 and 1895 various events interrupted the work of the subcommissions. In one case the Argentine head of the subcommission died and in another he was absent. In addition, complete disagreement on the demarcation principle prevented the writing of the required records of action when agreement on the specific site for the markers did occur. In this period the public press in both nations extended wide coverage to the boundary difficulties and displayed an extremely chauvinistic attitude. The press in each nation blamed the other country for lack of progress.

Two attempts to reach an agreement to resume demarcation in the last quarter of 1895 ended in failure. Chile was convinced that the only solution was arbitration, and she suggested it in February, 1896. At the same time Chile proposed that Argentina be given sovereignty over the Puna de Atacama in exchange for Chilean sovereignty in the Mount Aymond-Tres Montes area of the Strait. Argentina was willing to obtain sovereignty over the Puna de Atacama, but she would do no more than recognize the fact that Chile had presented a claim to the area near the Strait. In addition, Argentina would have limited arbitration by requiring that the boundary be restricted to the Cordillera of the Andes. Chile wanted to leave the arbitrator free to decide in accordance with the treaties. Continued discussion did produce another agreement in 1896.

The 1896 agreement extended boundary demarcation northward into the area Chile had obtained from Bolivia as a result of the War of the Pacific. [5] Inasmuch as the boundary had been in dispute between Argentina and Bolivia before the war, Bolivia was included in the direct negotiations. This agreement, too, contained a specific provision for arbitration. If any difference arose over demarcation, either nation or both could submit the matter to the arbitration of the British government sixty days after the difference arose. The marker at San Francisco Pass was not to be used as a precedent in the area north of the pass.

Soon after the agreement was signed, Argentine Expert Quirno P. Costa retired and was replaced by Sr. Francisco P. Moreno. The new expert did not arrive in Santiago until January, 1897. No demarcation occurred during his absence. Although Sr. Moreno attempted to accelerate the work of the commission, failure to agree upon the demarcation principle prevented any progress. Argentina insisted that the boundary follow the highest peaks, and Chile was equally insistent that the frontier should be determined by the water divide. Because neither country would yield, all the agreements and protocols concluded since the Boundary Treaty of 1881 had only postponed settlement.

Since 1878 Chile had been attempting to submit the boundary question to arbitration. Argentina, on the other hand, had been successfully demanding a direct settlement. The direct settlements that had been concluded, the Treaty of 1881 and the Protocols of 1888, 1893, and 1896, did not solve the problem. Because of the arbitration clauses in the Treaty of 1856, the Boundary Treaty of 1881, and the Protocol of 1896, Argentina could not refuse arbitration without repudiating those agreements; but until 1896 she had been successful in avoiding arbitration.

From the beginning of the boundary dispute the press in both countries had given wide coverage to events as they developed. As the matter dragged on and on, a more belligerent tone appeared on both sides of the Andes. The Argentine newspapers emphatically declared that the Treaty of 1881 provided for a boundary following the highest peaks and absolutely denied the validity of the water-parting line as a boundary. The Chilean press maintained that Argentina adhered to no one principle of demarcation but changed from one interpretation to another as individual cases arose in order to get the major portion of the disputed territory. By 1898 the press in both nations had aroused public opinion to the point of war. Because of the danger that the emotional trend of public opinion might push the two governments to the point of severing relations or even declaring war, a new and different agreement was concluded in the office of the president of Chile. This new proposal provided that each expert would draw a boundary line in accord with his interpretation of the Treaty of 1881. In August, 1898, the experts would present their lines to each other for comparison. In those areas where the experts agreed, the boundary would be marked. Those areas over which there was disagreement would be submitted to arbitration.

Between May and September each nation drew a boundary according to its interpretation of the Treaty of 1881. The two lines, when presented to the foreign ministers in September, did not agree. After each foreign minister certified that the line presented by the expert represented the position of his country, the boundary was divided into three sections. The northern section, extending from 23° through 26° 52' 45" south latitude, was the Puna de Atacama. This is the area Chile had earlier acquired from Bolivia. Since no attempt had been made to settle the boundary in this area, it was decided to continue direct negotiations. The middle section, the Andes-Patagonia area, stretched from the Puna de Atacama to 52° south. A list of boundary points upon which agreement existed and another list of disputed points were drawn up. The points of disagreement were submitted to the arbitration of the queen of England. The last section was the Strait boundary. Article two of the Treaty of 1881 established definite boundaries for this area; therefore, no problems of any significance existed in the Strait.

On November 2, 1898, Chile and Argentina conferred in Buenos Aires about the Puna de Atacama. They decided to establish a group composed of five delegates from each nation to decide the boundary by majority vote. The deliberations of the conference could consume no more than ten days or three sessions, and the decision of the group would not be binding on either government. If these ten men were unable to determine the boundary, a demarcation commission would assume the task of boundary determination. The demarcation commission would have three members: one appointed by Chile; one by Argentina; and the United States Minister in

Buenos Aires, William J. Buchanan. By majority vote the commission would decide the boundary and notify the Chilean and Argentine governments, who in turn would notify the Bolivian government. The demarcation commission was required under the terms of the agreement establishing it to meet within forty-eight hours after it was called and to complete the boundary work in three days.

All the necessary arrangements were completed by March, 1899. Each nation had appointed its five delegates,[6] and Mr. Buchanan had received permission from Secretary of State John Hay to accept appointment to the demarcation commission should it be needed. Mr. Buchanan had requested his government's permission even though he was acting as a private citizen.[7] The delegates met on the appointed day and unanimously approved rules of procedure which included majority vote, a quorum of ten, closed-door sessions, and two presidents presiding on alternate days. After reaching no agreement in two sessions, the commission met on March 9 in the last session. They voted to notify their respective governments of their failure and appointed two of their members, Sr. Enrique MacIver and Sr. José Uriburu, to the demarcation commission.

On November 21, 1899, forty-eight hours after they had been notified, the commissioners met in the Legation of the United States in Buenos Aires and within the allotted three days completed the delineation of the boundary. Both of the earlier lines suggested by the two governments were completely rejected in favor of a compromise suggested by Mr. Buchanan. The governments of Chile and Argentina accepted the work of the commission as the definitive boundary. The Puna de Atacama boundary was now settled. The Strait area boundary had been determined by the Treaty of 1881. Only the center section of the boundary between Argentina and Chile remained undecided, and this dispute had been submitted to arbitration by Queen Victoria.

Queen Victoria had accepted in July of 1896 the request of the governments of Chile and Argentina to arbitrate the boundary in the Patagonian Andes. More than two years later Prime Minister Lord Salisbury received a note from each government requesting the arbitration previously agreed upon. Queen Victoria then appointed an arbitration tribunal made up of a lawyer, Lord Edward Macnaghten, and three engineers; Major E. H. Hillis, Colonel Sir Thomas Hungerford Holdich, and Major General John C. Ardagh. Argentina presented her case with supporting documents to the president, Lord Macnaghten, in the middle of January, 1899, and Chile submitted her case shortly thereafter. Hearings continued until May. A few days after the hearings were completed, Argentina requested permission to present further evidence. The arbitration commission granted the

108

request and permitted Chile to reply to the countercase. Argentina did not give her two-part countercase to the tribunal until May and August, 1900, and the supporting documents were not delivered until December, 1900, and April, 1901. The Chilean reply was ready soon after.

In her case Chile argued that the controversial principle of demarcation included in article one of the Boundary Treaty of 1881 had to be included in the questions decided by the arbitrator because the arbitrator was required to base his decision upon the previous agreements, including that treaty. Argentina disagreed. Chile was absolutely correct. There was no way to avoid a decision on the demarcation principle if the arbitrator were required to use it to draw the boundary.

Argentina tried to avoid the problem by insisting that no problem existed. She based her case primarily upon a historical claim, and when she did mention the Treaty of 1881, she maintained there was no possible interpretation except the highest peaks of the Andes. The Argentine case justified the line the Argentine expert had delineated by presenting a historical review. Argentina claimed that not only had Patagonia and the Strait been placed under Buenos Aires by the Spanish king but that the colonial government had actually exercised control over the area. Argentina, as successor to the Viceroyalty of the Río de la Plata, succeeded to this authority. During the colonial period the term Chile, Argentina argued, included only the area of the Central Valley. Therefore, Chilean territory could not possibly be extended to the Strait. Furthermore, the Spanish sovereigns considered the Cordillera de los Andes as the natural and strategic frontier between the two parts of their empire. When the Viceroyalty of the Río de la Plata was created in 1776, the cordillera was made the boundary between it and the Captaincy General of Chile. The Cordillera de los Andes, Argentina said, had always meant the main chain of the Andes, and it was upon these peaks that the Argentine line had been based. Therefore, according to the uti posidetis of 1810, all of the area in dispute rightfully belonged to Argentina.

As far as the Treaty of 1881 was concerned, Argentina asserted, the negotiations had been based upon the highest peaks. There could be no question that at the time the treaty was written the intention of the two countries was to run the boundary line along the water divide of the highest peaks and not along the continental water divide. The continental water divide was never mentioned in the treaty. Argentina also insisted, contrary to fact, that the highest peaks are all in the main chain of the Andes. According to the Argentine case, the boundary determined by the arbitrator, who was limited to a decision in accord with the treaty, could not deviate from the highest peaks in the main chain of the Andes. The Argentine case went on to say that Chile's allegation charging Argentina with delaying the work of the experts by insisting upon surveys was unfounded. Demarcation under the Treaty of 1881 and the subsequent protocols and agreements was necessarily slow because a survey of the area had to be made in order to find the highest peaks of the main chain. Argentina had asked for no unnecessary delays, but the Chilean expert had stopped the process of demarcation by his disregard of international agreements.

Chile's reply answered each of the Argentine points. She advanced a claim to Patagonia and the Strait based upon the action of the Spanish kings during colonial times; so the uti posidetis of 1810 gave Chile these areas. During the negotiations for the Treaty of 1881, Chile maintained, a compromise had been arranged by which Chile had relinquished her claim to the northern part of Patagonia in return for an agreement to establish the continental water divide in the Andes as the boundary line. Article one of the Treaty of 1881 contains the statement of the agreement to establish the continental water divide as the principle of demarcation. The line proposed by Chile was based upon this principle; therefore, it represented the frontier as defined by the boundary agreements.

After examining the written cases and hearing the oral arguments, the arbitration tribunal decided to send a commission headed by one of its members, Colonel Sir Thomas H. Holdich, to study the actual geographic conditions of the Patagonian Andes. The commission included Captains C. L. Robertson, Bertran Dickson, W. H. Thompson, and Lieutenant H. A. Holdich. Between mid March and mid May the commission examined eight hundred miles of the border area to determine the feasibility of applying the Treaty of 1881 to the actual terrain. The commission then reported to the tribunal.

While the commission was in South America, relations between Chile and Argentina became strained; war seemed imminent. England exerted pressure on both countries to prevent war and hastened the arbitral award. On November 19, 1902, the arbitration tribunal handed its report to Edward VII, who had replaced Queen Victoria as arbitrator upon her death. The following day the king issued the award, which did not deviate from the recommendations of the tribunal. The decision did not adopt either of the proposed lines; instead, it established a compromise which awarded 15,450 square miles to Argentina and 20,850 square miles to Chile. The boundary marker in San Francisco Pass was placed upon the water divide, the point proposed by Chile. The area around Lake Lacar was granted to Argentina as well as most of the disputed area in the Pérez Rosales Pass section. The territory in the Última Esperanza district and in the Frías and the Aysen river valleys became Chilean.

The two countries seemed closer to war in 1902 than they actually were. Public opinion was greatly aroused in both, but the governments were actively working on agreements to restore harmonious relations. In a treaty signed April 30, 1900, they had drawn up a formula for the demarcation subcommissions to use in writing the record required at the erection of each boundary marker. The controversy over these records had been responsible for stopping the work of the subcommissions. In December of the same year a treaty providing for the maintenance of the status quo in the disputed area during arbitration peacefully settled another problem. One year later Argentina pledged her cooperation in marking the boundary.[10] Argentina's attempt to block the erection of markers had been greatly resented in Chile.

On May 28, 1902, Chile and Argentina signed three agreements designed to promote friendly relations in spite of the fact that at this time public opinion in both countries had been aroused by the press to such an extent that war seemed to be an immediate possibility.[11] One treaty requested the king of England to appoint a commission to mark the boundary when it had been determined by the award. King Edward consented and appointed the men making up the arbitration commission which had explored the southern portion of the frontier in March, April, and May of that year. Another agreement provided for arbitration by England of any differences that might arise between the two nations. The third treaty was an arms limitation agreement.

The treaties signed in May, 1902, and the award handed down in November mollified public opinion and greatly improved relations between the two countries. The causes of the dispute had been removed. All the major disagreements over the Chilean-Argentine boundary line from the Puna de Atacama to Cape Horn had been settled by a combination of direct agreement and arbitration by England and the United States. Between 1903 and 1905 additional treaties settled the remaining differences over demarcation of the line already established, and the king of England was again asked to act as arbitrator, this time to settle any difficulties which might arise in the demarcation of the line in the Puna de Atacama.

In 1903 only one minor disagreement over boundary determination remained, the question of sovereignty over the islands in the Beagle Channel. The three largest of the disputed islands, Picton, Nueva, and Lennox, are located at the eastern entrance of the channel that runs between the southern coast of Tierra del Fuego and Navarino Island. Article three of the Boundary Treaty of 1881 divided Tierra del Fuego from Cape Espíritu Santo to the Beagle Channel along the 68° 34' longitude line. The islands east of Tierra del Fuego belonged to Argentina; those south of the Beagle

Channel and west of Tierra del Fuego belonged to Chile

The point in dispute was the location of the eastern entrance to the channel. Chile maintained that the channel ran north of all three islands; consequently, she claimed and exercised sovereignty over them. Argentina, on the other hand, declared that Picton, Nueva, and perhaps Lennox were situated within the channel and pressed her claim to Picton and Nueva. She was willing to discuss the Lennox situation further.

Argentina had presented her claim to these islands to the arbitration tribunal in 1902, but the treaty submitting the dispute to arbitration limited the scope of arbitration to that portion of the boundary between 26° 52' 45" S. and 52° S. Therefore, the King's Award did not mention the disputed islands. In 1905 Argentina invited Chile to mark the mouth of the Beagle Channel, but this suggestion was not acted upon. Chile was exercising sovereignty over the three islands, and she continued to do so.

Not until 1915 did Argentina again press her claim to the islands. Argentina's renewed interest in the islands was the result of a decree issued by the Chilean Minister of Foreign Relations, Religion, and Colonization. Decree number 2008 dated December 15, 1914, granted Mariano Edwards Ariztéa permission to occupy Picton, Nueva, and six smaller islands nearby for an additional fifteen years.[12] Since 1902 these islands had been granted to Chileans by the Chilean government without any protest from Argentina. However, when in March of 1915 Argentina learned of the Edwards Ariztéa grant, she protested to Chile; and the two nations entered into discussions about the disputed islands.

On June 28 representatives of the two countries signed a treaty submitting the question of sovereignty over the Beagle Channel Islands to the arbitration of the king of England. Both contracting parties would request arbitration in a note signed jointly. The arbitrator would decide the question on the basis of the treaties in force at the time of the request. Although Lennox Island was not consistently claimed by Argentina, Chile agreed to include it in the arbitration; for she felt her claim to it and to the other islands was clear and just.

The joint note requesting arbitration was never signed; the wording of the note could not be agreed upon. Argentina preferred a direct settlement, but a direct settlement could not be reached. The question was not of major importance, and it was dropped as other events such as World War I and the subsequent depression engaged the attention of Chile and Argentina. During this period both nations were also experiencing domestic problems. Economic readjustments and political instability plagued them both.

After some time the two did resume their efforts to settle the remaining boundary issue. Another arbitration treaty was signed on May 4, 1938.[13] By the terms of the treaty Homer S. Cummings, Attorney General of the United States, was appointed arbitrator to decide which country would receive the Beagle Channel Islands. He would make his decision on the basis of the existing treaties after being requested to act as arbitrator by a joint note.

In January, 1939, Mr. Cummings resigned his position as Attorney General; so he was not requested to act as arbitrator. The arbitration was postponed indefinitely. There was some talk about making other arrangements for arbitration, but Argentina still favored a direct settlement. Chile was not anxious to do anything; the islands were in Chile's possession.

World War II distracted the two nations until 1945; then, post-war political and economic readjustments claimed their attention. In the last half of the decade of the 1940's, Chile was preoccupied with loss of markets, inflation, and strikes as well as the political instability caused by the death of President Juan Antonio Ríos in office and the attempt of the new president, Gabriel González Videla, to include the resurgent communists in his government.

Juan Peron seized power in Argentina in October, 1945, and had himself elected to the office of president in February, 1946. During the Peron regime, which lasted until his exile in 1955, Argentina was completely engaged in the implementation of Peron's program for what he regarded as a sweeping reform of Argentina's political, economic, and social structures.

In 1954 Chile established Puerto Williams on Navarino Island to serve as a command post for the disputed area and began maintaining a small, permanent naval station at that location. Argentina reacted to Chilean activity in the Beagle Channel area in August, 1958, by destroying an automatic beacon on Snipe Island, close to the Atlantic entrance to the Beagle Channel. Two days later Argentina landed eighty sailors to seize control of the island. Chile withdrew her ambassador in Buenos Aires. Public opinion in Chile was becoming increasingly anti-Argentine. Students paraded in the streets of Santiago demanding vigorous action against Argentina. Argentina proposed arbitration of the dispute. In a personal message sent to Chilean President Carlos Ibañez, President Arturo Frondizi initiated discussions of the issue at the highest level. Pending settlement, both nations agreed to withdraw all forces and abandon all activity on Snipe Island.

An increased interest by both countries in greater economic cooperation led to a meeting in February, 1959, between President Frondizi and the new Chilean president, Jorge Alessandri. In a joint statement the presidents agreed to economic cooperation and suitable arbitration of the remaining border disputes, but an arbitration accord was not reached at that time.

During the last half of 1959 additional border incidents occurred in the Beagle Channel area, on the frontier near the Puna de Atacama, and in the Palena Valley near Chiloé. In March of 1960 the governments of Chile and Argentina announced an agreement to submit the Beagle Channel and Palena Valley disputes to the International Court of Justice for arbitration, but the request was never sent to the Court. Argentina then proposed arbitration by Great Britain. On March 29 both nations made public the text of two proposed treaties settling the boundary disputes and the problem of naval activity in the Strait. The Palena Valley dispute was given to Queen Elizabeth II to settle; the Tierra del Fuego disagreement was given to the International Court of Justice to settle; and it was agreed that any future border disputes would be sent to the president of Switzerland.

Although Queen Elizabeth agreed to act as arbitrator in May, an attempt to reach a direct settlement began in July; and ratification of the arbitration treaties was not exchanged. The direct negotiations were not successful, and the border incidents were becoming more serious. By July, 1964, tensions in Chile were aroused to such a high degree that all of the previous agreements were in danger. Numerous rumors with political overtones were circulating. Salvador Allende, leader of the leftist political coalition, accused the rightist of plotting with the Argentine military to effect a coup to prevent the leftists from coming to power in Chile. There was also a rumor that the recently concluded United States-Argentine military assistance agreement provided for cooperation between the military forces of Argentina and the United States to oppose the leftist coalition should it win the presidential elections in Chile.

In an attempt to remove the border dispute from politics, President Alessandri in August of 1964 requested Queen Elizabeth to arbitrate the boundary disagreements. On November 6 Argentina announced that she would agree to British arbitration of the Palena Valley dispute and to arbitration by the International Court of Justice for the Beagle Channel area. However, no further action was taken by either nation at that time.

One year later the first death since the King's Award had been signed in 1902 took place as the result of a border conflict. An Argentine border patrol engaged a Chilean border post at Laguna del Desierto, fifty miles north of Punta Arenas. One Chilean border guard was killed and three guards, one of whom was wounded, were taken prisoner. Students from the University of Chile demonstrated in the streets of Santiago, and the Argentine embassy was stoned. The government sent planes loaded with heavily armed police to the area, and congress went into secret, emergency session. The chief of the armed forces was called home from the continental defense conference in Lima.

Even though public opinion in Chile was aroused to a war fever, the government responded favorably to assurances given by the Argentine government. However, neither country would accept responsibility for the border incident that had resulted in the death of the guard. Nevertheless, President Eduardo Frei of Chile and President Arturo Illia of Argentina were anxious to prevent any future trouble and agreed to withdraw from the disputed territory pending demarcation of the boundary. Both presidents were subject to increasing pressure from public opinion and from the military. President Illia had a very difficult time restraining the military in his country. The Argentine military was more nationalistic than Chile's because of the Argentine expansion program in the Strait area and in Antarctica. Tension eased in December, 1965, when a joint border commission was established to mark the boundary in the Laguna del Desierto region. President Illia and President Frei moderated their demands to effect a rapid settlement in order to prevent the military from gaining control of the situation.

On December 29, 1965, delegates of Argentina and Chile appeared before the British arbitration tribunal in London. Each country stated its case in the Palena Valley dispute. One year later the British court of arbitration announced its ruling. Argentina received the larger portion of the valley, which is twenty-four miles long, but Chile obtained the area in which her nationals lived. Both nations accepted the decision.

In December, 1967, a year after the successful arbitration by England of the Palena Valley problem, Chile requested English arbitration of the dispute over the Beagle Channel Islands. Argentina denied any knowledge of the Chilean request and declared both England and Elizabeth II unacceptable as arbitrator. Initially no explanation was given. Six months later Argentina explained that England was prejudiced against her because of the dispute that Argentina had been having with England over the Falkland Islands since 1832, a fact which had not seemed important to Argentina during the earlier arbitrations.

During the first week in May, 1968, a serious war scare developed. Using jet aircraft, aircraft carriers, submarines, cruisers, and patrol boats, the air force and navy of both nations began operating in the Beagle Channel. Such activity created the imminent danger of another incident.

Argentina claimed that knowledge discovered since the demarcation of Tierra del Fuego in 1893 placed the channel south of three disputed islands in the mouth of the Beagle Channel, making them Argentine. Chile charged that Argentina was attempting to strengthen her claim to Antarctica by extending Argentine sovereignty south to Antarctica across the Drake Passage. The military in Argentina viewed the Chilean presence in the Beagle Channel as a threat to the Argentine naval base at Ushuaia on the southern coast of Tierra del Fuego. Argentina was worried also about the fact that forty-two percent of the population in the Argentine portion of Tierra del Fuego was Chilean.

In July, 1971, Salvador Allende, now president of Chile, and President Alejandro Lanusse of Argentina met in Salta, Argentina, and agreed on a solution for the Beagle Channel dispute. Queen Elizabeth II was given responsibility for deciding the boundary, using as the basis of her award a technical decision rendered by a five member court made up of the judges of the World Court in The Hague. The Argentine government changed its mind in March of the following year. The Argentine foreign ministry announced that Argentina was withdrawing from the 1902 treaty, which had provided for arbitration. The 1902 treaty provided that either nation, after giving six months notice, could withdraw at the end of each ten-year period. Argentina maintained that the treaty had to be brought up to date and new ways of solving international disputes had to be found. Previous arrangements for settling the disagreement over the Beagle Channel were no longer acceptable. Internal political and economic problems are the primary concern of both governments at the present time. Nothing is being done on the Beagle Channel dispute, and the problem in the area of the Puna de Atacama seems to have been forgotten, at least temporarily.

NOTES

1. Appendix to the Statement Presented on Behalf of Chile, 1, p. 4.
2. The documents are printed in Alejandro Bertrand, Estudio Tecnico acerca de la aplicación de las reglas para la demarcación de limites i especialmente del limite en la cordillera de los Andes, segun se halla estipulado en las convenios internacionales entre Chile i la República Arjentina (Santiago: Imprenta Cervantes, 1895).
3. Bertrand, Estudio Tecnico, pp. 123-126.
4. Statement Presented on Behalf of Chile, 2, pp. 450-455.
5. Bascuñan Montes, Recopilación, 3, pp. 314-320.
6. The Chilean delegates were Eulogio Altamirano, Rafael Balmaceda,

Enrique Mac-Iver, Eduardo Matte, and Luis Pereira. The Argentine delegates were Bernardo de Irigoyen, Bartolomé Mitre, Juan José Romero, José E. Uriburu, and Benjamin Victorica.

7. See Papers Relating to the Foreign Relations of the United States, 1898.
8. See Thomas H. Holdich, The Countries of the King's Award (London: Hurst and Blackett, Limited, 1904).
9. The report of the arbitration tribunal and the award are printed in Bascuñan Montes, Recopilación, 6, pp. 20-38.
10. Bascuñan Montes, Recopilación, 5, pp. 251-253, 271-274.
11. Bascuñan Montes, Recopilación, 6, pp. 10-19, 50-55, 59-60.
12. Diario oficial de la República de Chile, 34, (January 26, 1915), pp. 381-382.
13. Chile, Memoria del Ministerio de Relaciones Esteriores 1938, pp. 334-338.

BIBLIOGRAPHY

This bibliography is not intended to be a complete survey of all the literature concerned with the Chilean boundaries. The works included are those that have been useful for this study.

GENERAL WORKS

Histories: Diego Barros Arana, Historia jeneral de Chile, 16 vols. (Santiago, 1884-1902) and Historia de America and Estudios Históricos, Vols. I and VII of Obras Completas (Santiago, 1879-1881). Isaiah Bowman, Desert Trails of Atacama (New York, 1924). Robert J. Casey, Easter Island: Home of the Scornful Gods (Indianapolis, 1931). Francisco A. Encina, Historia de Chile desde la prehistoria hasta 1891, 15 vols. (Santiago, 1941-1950). Luis Galdames, Historia de Chile: La Evolución constitucional (Santiago, 1925). Jorge Guzman Parada, Cumbres Oceánicas (las Islas Juan Fernández) (Santiago, 1950). William H. Prescott, Peru, 2 vols. (New York, 1901-1902).

Boundary Studies: S. Whittemore Boggs, International Boundaries - A Study of Boundary Functions and Problems (New York, 1940). Gordon Ireland, Boundaries, Possessions, and Conflicts in South America (Cambridge, Mass., 1938). Alexander Marchant, Boundaries of the Latin American Republics: An Annotated List of Documents 1493-1943 (Tentative Version) (Washington, D. C., 1944). Juan Angulo Puente Arnao, Historia de los límites del Perú (Lima, 1927). Ramon Serrano Montaner, Límites con la República Arjentina (Santiago, 1898). Luis V. Varela, Histoire de la Démarcation des leurs Frontieres (depuis 1843 jusqu'a 1899), 2 vols. (Buenos Aires, 1899).

Diplomacy: William Miller Collier and Feliú Guillermo Cruz, La primera Mision de los Estados Unidos de America en Chile (Santiago, 1926).

Vicente G. Quesada, Historia diplomatica Latino-America, 3 vols. (Buenos Aires, 1918-1920). Alejandro Alavrez, Rasgos general de la historia diplomática de Chile (1810-1910): Primera Epoca, la Emancipación (Santiago, 1911). Centro de Estudios de Derecho Internacional, La Politica Exterior de la Republica Argentina (Buenos Aires, 1931). Adolfo Calderón Cousiño, Short Diplomatic History of the Chilean-Peruvian Relations (Santiago, 1920). Ernesto Quesada, La Politica Chilena en el Plata (Buenos Aires, 1895).

COLONIAL PERIOD

Documents: Manuel de Amat y Junient, Memoria de Gobierno (Sevilla, 1947). Roberto Levillier, Gobernación del Tucumán correspondencia de los cabildos en el siglo XVI (Madrid, 1918). José Toribio Medina, Cartas de Pedro de Valdivia que tratan del descubrimiento y conquista de Chile (Sevilla, 1929). José Toribio Medina, Colección de Documentos Inéditos para la Historia de Chile desde el Viaje de Magallanes Hasta la Batalla de Maipo 1518-1818, 30 vols. (Santiago, 1888-1902). José Toribio Medina, Coleccion de historiadores de Chile y de documentos relativos a la historia nacional, 45 vols. (Santiago, 1861-1923). Marquis de Miraflores and Miguel Salva, Colección de documentos ineditos para la historia de España, 113 vols. (Madrid, 1842-1895). Ulrich Schmidt, A true and agreeable description of some principal Indian lands and islands... (London, 1891). Luis Torres de Mendoza, Colección de Documentos Inéditos relativos al descubrimiento, conquista y organización de la antigua posesiones españolas de America y Oceania..., 42 vols. (Madrid, 1864-1884).

Biographies and Histories: Rosa Arciniega, Don Pedro de Valdivia, Conquistador de Chile (Santiago, 1943). Bolton Glanville Corney, The Voyages of Captain Don Felipe Gonzalez... (Cambridge, 1908). Crescente Errázuriz, Historia de Chile: Francisco de Villagra 1561-1563 (Santiago, 1915). Crescente Errázuriz, Historia de Chile: Pedro de Valdivia, 2 vols. (Santiago, 1912). Crescente Errázuriz, Historia de Chile sin gobernador 1554-1557 (Santiago, 1912). R. B. Cunningham Graham, Pedro de Valdivia. Conqueror of Chile (London, 1926). Clements R. Markham, The Voyages of Pedro Fernandez de Quiros 1595 to 1606, 2 vols. (London, 1904). José T. Medina, El piloto Juan Fernández... (Santiago, 1943). Vicente Rodriguez Casada and Florentino Perez Embid, Construcciones Militares del Virrey Amat (Sevilla, 1949). Juan Luis Espejo, La Provincia de Cuyo del Reino de Chile, 2 vols. (Santiago, 1954). Ricardo Jaimes Freyre, El Tucumán Colonial... (Buenos Aires, 1915). Enrique de Gandia, Historia de

119

la conquista del Río de la Plata y del Paraguay... (Buenos Aires, 1932). Roberto Levillier, Nueva crónica de la conquista del Tucumán, 3 vols. (Buenos Aires, 1926-1930). Manuel Lizondo Borda, Historia de la Gobernación del Tucumán (siglo XVI) (Buenos Aires, 1928). Vicente G. Quesada, Vireinato del Río de la Plata 1776-1810... (Buenos Aires, 1881). Antonio Zinny, Historia de los Gobernadores de las Provincias Argentina, 5 vols. (Buenos Aires, 1920-1921).

NATIONAL PERIOD - DOCUMENTS

Chile: Ricardo Anguita, Leyes Promulgadas en Chile desde 1810 hasta el 1 de Junio de 1812 (Santiago, 1912). Aurelio Bascuñan Montes and others, Recopilación de Tratados, Convenciones, Protocolos y otros Actos Internacionales celebradas por la República de Chile, 6 vols. (Santiago, 1894-1913). Constitucion Politica de la República de Chile Jurada y Promulgada el 25 de Mayo de 1833 con las Reformas efectuadas hasta el 26 de Junio de 1893 (Santiago, 1909). English translation by C. W. Tooke (Urbana, Ill., 1899). República de Chile, Diario oficial de la República de Chile. Republica de Chile, Memoria del Ministerio de Relaciones Exteriores y comercio correspondiente al año 1938 (Santiago, 1941). Paul V. Shaw, The Early Constitutions of Chile 1810-1833 (New York, 1930). Javier Vial Solar, Los Tratados de Chile, 2 vols. (Santiago, 1903).

Peru: Ricardo Aranda, Colección de los Tratados, convenciones, capitulaciones, armisticios y otros actos diplomáticos y politicos celebrados desde la independencia hasta el dia..., 14 vols. (Lima, 1890). República de Peru, Ministerio de Relaciones Exteriores, Colección de los Tratados, Convenciones, Capitulaciones, Armisticios y otros actos diplomáticos y politicos celebrados desde la Independencia hasta el Dia, precedida de una introducción que comprende la época colonial, 14 vols. (Lima, 1890-1911).

Argentina: República de Argentina, Memoria de Relaciones Exteriores y Culto 1899, 1902-1903, 1915-1916 (Buenos Aires). República de Argentina, Ministro del Interior, Los Tratados de Paz de 1902 ante el Congreso (Buenos Aires, 1904). República de Argentina, Tratados, Convenciones, Protocolos, Actos y Acuerdos Internacionales, 11 vols. (Buenos Aires, 1911-1912).

BOLIVIAN BOUNDARY

Luis Barros Borgoño, The Problem of the Pacific and the New Policies of Bolivia (Baltimore, 1924). Victor M. Maurtua, The Question of the Pacific (New York, 1927). Miguel Mercado M., Historia Internacional de Bolivia Cuestion de límites (1916). Emilio Bello Codocido, Anotaciones para la historia de las negociaciones diplomáticos con el Peru y Bolivia 1900-1904 (Santiago, 1919). Documentos oficiales relativos a los límites entre Chile, Bolivia i la República Arjentina en la rejion de Atacama (Santiago, 1898). Alejandro Fierro, Cuestion Chileno-Boliviana. Exposición del Ministro de Relaciones Esteriores de Chile sobre los motivos que justifican la reivindicacion del territorio comprendio entre los paralelos 23 y 24 latitud sur (Valparaiso, 1879). República de Chile, Oficina de Mensura de Tierras, La línea de Frontera con la República de Bolivia (Santiago, 1910).

WAR OF THE PACIFIC

Pascual Ahumada Moreno, Guerra del Pacifico Récopilación completa de todos los documentos oficiales, correspondencias i demas publicaciones referentes a la guerra que ha dado a luz la prensa de Chile, Peru i Bolivia conteniendo documentos inéditos de importancia, 8 vols. (Valparaiso, 1884-1891). Diego Barros Arana, Historia de la Guerra del Pacifico (Obras Completas, vol. 16). Gonzalo Bulnes, Chile and Peru: The Causes of the War of 1879 (Santiago, 1920). Gonzalo Bulnes, Guerra del Pacifico, 3 vols. (Valparaiso, 1912-1919). Tomás Gaivano, Historia de la Guerra de la America entre Chile, Peru y Bolivia, 3 vols. (Lima, 1901-1904). Alberto Gutiérrez, La Guerra de 1879 (Paris, 1914). C. A. Logan and F. G. Calderón, Mediacion de los Estados Unidos de Norte Americana en la Guerra del Pacifico (Buenos Aires, 1884). Clements R. Markham, The War Between Chile and Peru 1879-1882 (London, 1882). Benjamin Vicuña MacKenna, Guerra del Pacifico: Historia de la campaña de Tacna y Arica 1879-1880 (Santiago, 1881).

TACNA - ARICA

Documents: Arbitration Between Peru and Chile: the Memorial of Peru and the Ruling and Observations of the Arbitrator (In English and Spanish) (Washington, D.C., 1925). Arbitration Between Peru and Chile:

The Case of Peru in the Matter of the Controversy arising out of the Question of the Pacific before the President of the United States Arbitrator under the Protocol and supplementary Act between the Republic of Peru and the Republic of Chile, signed July 20, 1922 at Washington, D. C., ratified January 15, 1923 (Washington, D. C., 1923). Arbitration Between Peru and Chile: Appendix to the Case of Peru... (Washington, D. C., 1923). Arbitration Between Peru and Chile: The Counter Case of Peru... (Washington, D. C., 1923). Arbitration Between Peru and Chile: Appendix to the Counter Case of Peru... (Washington, D. C., 1923). William Jefferson Dennis, "Documentary History of the Tacna-Arica Dispute." University of Iowa Studies in the Social Sciences, vol. 8, no. 3. In the Matter of the Arbitration Between the Republic of Chile and the Republic of Peru, with regard to the unfulfilled Provisions of the Treaty of Peace of October 20, 1883, under the Protocol and Supplementary Act Signed at Washington July 20, 1922, Opinion and Award of the Arbitrator (Washington, D. C., 1925). República de Chile, Ministerio de Relaciones Exteriores de Chile, Comunicaciones cambiadas entre las cancillerías de Chile y Peru y algunos antecedentes sobre la cuestión de Tacna y Arica (1905 a 1910) (Santiago, 1912). "Tacna-Arica Arbitration" American Journal of International Law, vol. 20 (1920). Tacna-Arica Arbitration: The Case of the Republic of Chile submitted to the President of the United States as Arbitrator under the Provisions of the Protocol and Supplementary Agreement Entered Into Between Chile and Peru at Washington on July 20, 1922 (Washington, D. C., 1923). Tacna-Arica Arbitration: The Appendix to the Case of the Republic of Chile... (Washington, D. C., 1923). Tacna-Arica Arbitration: The Counter-Case of the Republic of Chile... (Washington, D. C., 1924). Tacna-Arica Arbitration: The Appendix to the Counter-Case of the Republic of Chile... (Washington, D. C., 1924). Tacna-Arica Arbitration: Notes on the Peruvian Case and Appendix submitted with the Counter-Case of the Republic of Chile to the President... (Washington, D. C., 1924).

Secondary Works: Luis Aldunate, Los Tratados de 1883-84 a proposito de las declaraciones del Mensaje presidencial de 1 de junio en curso (Santiago, 1912). Victor Andrés Belaunde, Nuestra cuestion con Chile (Lima, 1919). Victor Andrés Belaunde, The Treaty of Ancon in the Light of International Law (Washington, D. C., 1927). Ernesto Barros Jarpa, Hacia la solución: Apuntaciones al margen de la negociación chileno-peruana de 1921 (Santiago, 1922). Rafael Egaña, La Cuestión de Tacna i Arica Antecedentes Historicos Jestiones Dipolmáticas Estado actual (Santiago, 1900). Luis Orrego Luce, Los problemas internacionales de Chile: La cuestion El Tratado de 1881 y negociaciones posteriores (Santiago, 1902).

El Problema de Tacna y Arica: encuesta de La Nacion de Buenos Aires: opiniones de los Señores: Don Antonio Hunceus, José Miguel Echeñique, Javier Vial Solar, Julio Pérez Cante, Paulino Altonso, Guillermo Pérez de Arce, Gonzalo Bulnes, Frederico Puga Borne, Malaquias Concha, Anselmo Blanlot Holley, Alamiro Huidobro (Santiago, 1919). William Jefferson Dennis, Tacna and Arica: An Account of the Chile-Peru Boundary Dispute and of the Arbitration by the United States (New Haven, 1931). Graham H. Stuart, "The Tacna-Arica Dispute" World Peace Foundation Pamphlets, vol. 10, no. 1 (1927).

THE STRAIT AREA

Colonial Period: Alonso (Veedor), "Narrative of Events which Happened in the Fleet of Simon de Alcazaba who went out as Governor of the Province of Leon in the Parts of the South Sea. Having to Pass the Strait of Magellan. He took two ships, the capitana called Madre de Dios and the Other called San Pedro in which were embarked, including passangers and sailors, 250 persons." Translated by Clements Markham in Early Spanish Voyages to the Strait of Magellan, Hakluyt Society Publications, series 2, vol. 28 (London, 1911). Pablo Pastells, El Descubrimiento del Estrecho de Magallanes en conmemoración del IV centenario, 2 vols. (Madrid, 1920). Pedro Sarmiento de Gamboa, Viajes al Estrecho de Magallanes 1579-1584, 2 vols. (Buenos Aires, 1950).

Chilean Colonization: Nicolas Anrique Reyes, Diario de la Goleta "Ancud" al mando del Capitan de Fragata don Juan Guillermos (1843) Para tomar posesion del Estrecho de Magallanes (Santiago, 1901). Julius Beerbohm, Wanderings in Patagonia or Life Among the Ostrich-Hunters (London, 1881). Charles Brown, Insurrection at Magellan. Narrative of the Imprisonment and Escape of Capt. Chas. H. Brown, from the Chilean Convicts (Boston, 1854). Armando Braun Menéndez, Fuerte Bulnes: Historia de la ocupación del Estrecho de Magallanes por el Gobierno de Chile en 1843, precedida de una Crónica somera de aquel paso de mar y los antecedentes de la expedición; viaje de la goleta "Ancud", fundación del Fuerte Bulnes y secesos ocurridos hasta el translado de la colonia a Punta Arenas en 1849 (Buenos Aires, 1943). Armando Braun Menéndez, Pequeña Historia Magallánica las cuatro fundaciones Magallánicas, crónicas del antiguo Punta Arenas, el abrazo del Estrecho con ilustraciones de Juan Pablo Laverdet ejecutadas según documentos originales (Buenos Aires, 1945). Charles Darwin, Charles Darwin's Diary of the Voyage of H. M. S. "Bea-

123

gle" (New York, 1933). Ernesto Grave, "Los primeros años de la Coloni-
zacion del Estrecho de Magallanes: sus lecciones para el futuro," Revista
Chilena de Historia y Geografía, vol. 75, no. 82 (May-August, 1934).
Philip Parker King, Robert Fitz-Roy, and Charles Darwin, Narratives of
the Surveying Voyages of His Majesty's Ships Adventure and Beagle, between the years 1826 and 1836, describing their Examination of the Southern
Shores of South America, and the Beagle's Circumnavigation of the Globe,
3 vols. (London, 1839)..

CHILEAN-ARGENTINE ARBITRATION

Documents: Argentine-Chilean Boundary Report presented to the
Tribunal Appointed by Her Britannic Majesty's Government "To consider
and report upon the differences which have arisen with regard to the frontier between the Argentine and Chilean Republics" to justify the Argentine
claims for the boundary in the summit of the Cordillera de los Andes, according to the Treaties of 1881 & 1893, 5 vols. (London, 1900). Statement
Presented on Behalf of Chile in Reply to the Argentine Report submitted to
the Tribunal Constituted by H. B. Majesty's Government acting as Arbitrator in pursuant of the Agreement dated April 17, 1896, 4 vols. (London,
1901-1902). Appendix to the Statement Presented on Behalf of Chile..., 2
vols. (London, 1902). Demarcacion de Límites entre Chile i la República
Arjentina: Tratados i Protocolos vijantes, Actas i comunicaciones oficiales relativas a la linea jeneral de Frontera (Santiago, 1898). República
de Chile, Oficina de Límites, La Cordillera de los Andes las Latitudes 30º
40' i 35º S. Trabajos i Estudios de la Segunda Subcomision Chilena de Límites con la República Arjentina con gráficos, mapas i Fotograbados (Santiago, 1903). República de Chile, Oficina de Límites, La Cordillera de los
Andes entre las Latitudes 46º i 50º S. con gráficos, i mapa, i 10 Fotograbados (Santiago, 1905). República de Chile, Oficina de Límites, La Linea
de Frontera con la República Arjentina entre las Latitudes 35º i 46º S.
segun los Trabajos de diversas Sub-comisiones, a cargo de los injenieros
señores Anibal Contreras P., Cárlos Soza B., Alvaro Donoso G., Ernesto Frick J., Cárlos Aguirre L., Cárlos Barrios M., i Victor Caro T.
con dos planos, dos gráficos i diez Fotograbados (Santiago, 1907). República de Chile, Oficina de Límites, La Linea de Frontera con la República
Arjentina entre las Latitudes 27º i 30º S. segun los Trabajos de la Subcomision Chilena de Límites con la República Arjentina a cargo del inje-
niero don Cárlos Soza B. con un gráfico, un mapa i cuatro Fotograbados
(Santiago, 1907). República de Chile, Oficina de Límites, Memoria sobre

la Demarcación Arbitral de Límites entre Chile i la República de Arjentina Acompañada de una lista enumerativa de todos los puntos de la línea fronteriza desde el Paso de San Francisco (Copiapó) hasta el Canal Beagle (Tierra del Fuego), presentada al Ministerio de Relacciones Esteriores por el perito de Chile i de los informes del Delegado Arbitral de S. M. B. i de su Ayudantes con 27 planos (Santiago, 1904).

Secondary Works: Miguel Luis Amunátagui, La cuestion de límites entre Chile i la República Arjentina, 3 vols. (Santiago, 1879-1880). Pedro de Angelis, Memoria Historica sobre los Derechos de Soberania y Dominio de la Confederación Argentina a la parte austral del continente Americano, comprendida entre las costas del Oceano Atlantico y la gran cordillera de los Andes, desde la boca del Río de la Plata hasta el Cabo de Hornos, inclusa la isla de los Estados, la Tierra del Fuego, y el Estrecho de Magallanes en su extension (Buenos Aires, 1852). Eduardo de la Barra, Cartas a un Senador de la República (Valparaiso, 1896). Eduardo de la Barra, El problema de los Andes (Buenos Aires, 1895). Alejandro Bertrand (Chilean member of the Demarcation Commission), Estudio Tecnico acerca de la aplicación de demarcación de límites i especialmente del límite en la cordillera de los Andes, según se halla estipulado en los convenios internacionales entre Chile i la República Argentina (Santiago, 1895). Enrique S. Delachaux (Argentine Expert), El articulo del Dr. Juan Steffan: La Cuestion de límites Chileno-Argentina con especial consideracion de la Patagonia: Exámen critico (La Plata, 1898). Joaquín González, Los Tratados de Paz de 1902 Ante el Congreso (Buenos Aires, 1904). J. Guillermo Guerra, La soberano Chilena en las Islas al sur del Canal Beagle (Santiago, 1917). Thomas H. Holdich (Member of the Arbitration Commission), The Countries of the King's Award (London, 1904). Bernardo de Irigoyen, Question des Limites entre la République Argentine et le Chili (Buenos Aires, 1881). Manuel Augusta Montes de Oca, Limites avec le Chile ce que l'on voit, et ce que l'on ne voit pas L'Arbitrage La Puna D'Atacama (Buenos Aires, 1898). Henri-Alexis Moulin, Le Litige Chilo-Argentin et la Délimitation Politique de Frontieres Naturelles (Paris, 1902). Ernesto Quesada, La politica Argentina Respecto de Chile (1895-1898) (Buenos Aires, 1898). Hans Steffen, Viajes de Esploración i estudio en la Patagonia Occidental 1892-1902, 2 vols. (Santiago, 1909-1910). Luis V. Varela, La Puna de Atacama Su situación ante la Conferencias Internacional de los delegados de las Repúblicas Argentina y Chile (Buenos Aires, 1899). Estanislao S. Zeballos, Demarcación de límites entre la República Argentina y Chile Extracto de la Memoria presentada al Congreso de la Nacion (Buenos Aires, 1902).

Abascal, Fernando de, 23
Aconcagua province, 27
Alcazaba, Simón de, 3, 4, 5, 9; early career, 3-4; expedition to Strait, 5-6
Adventure, 33, 78; voyages, 73-75
Alderate, Jerónimo de, 13
Aldunate, Carlos, 64
Aldunate, Luis, 55, 56
Alessandri, Jorge, 113, 114
Allende, Salvador, 114, 116
Almagro, Diego de, 4, 5, 10, 11; expedition to Chile, 10
Almirante Cochrane, 48
Alto Peru, 3
Alvarado, Gomez de, 10
Amat y Junyent Planella Aymerich y Sant Pau, Manuel de, 15
Ancón, Treaty of, 53-55, 56, 57, 61, 62, 63, 64, 65, 66, 67, 69, 70
Ancud, 85; construction and voyage to Strait, 79-83
Ancud, San Carlos de, 23, 78, 79 81, 83, 84; Gulf, 93
Andreu y Guerrero, Rafael, Bishop 15
Angamos, Battle of, 47
Antarctica, 77, 115, 116
Antofagasta, city, 39, 42, 43, 44, 45, 46; province, 48, 49, 52, 56, 57, 58
Antofagasta Railroad and Nitrate Company, 42, 43, 44, 45
Apodaca, Exequiel, 44
Araucanian Indians, 12
Arauco province, 30
arbitration.by Queen Victoria, 108-110
arbitration by United States, 66-67
Ardagh, John C., 108
Arequipa, 15, 53, 55

Argentina, 13, 33, 36, 41, 62, 73, 74, 84, 87, 88, 90, 91, 92, 93, 95, 96, 98, 99, 101, 102, 105, 106, 107, 108, 109, 110, 111, 112, 113, 114, 115, 116
Argentine Confederation, 91, 92
Arias, Juan, 5
Arica, city, 46, 47, 57, 59, 68, 70; province, 48, 52, 53, 54, 55, 56, 57, 58, 61, 62, 65, 67, 68, 69, 70; bay, 52; Morro of, 70
Arica-La Paz Railroad, 59, 70
Army of the Andes (San Martín), 25
Ash, Benjamin, 81, 82
Atacama, Desert of, 3, 10, 11, 15, 26, 27, 28, 29, 33, 34, 43, 73; province, 30, 32
Atahualpa, 46
Atlantic Ocean, 5, 14, 74, 93, 104
Australia, 75
Avellaneda, Nicolás, 94
Aysen River, 110
Badajos Conference, March, 1524, 3
Bahia, Brazil, 8
Balmaceda, José, 61, 102
Baquedano, Manuel, 49
Barros, Diego Antonio, 77
Barros Arana, Diego, 94, 95, 102-105
Bayonne, France, 9, 18
Beagle, 33, 78; voyages, 73-75
Beagle Channel, 94, 98, 111-112, 113, 114, 115, 116
Beagle Channel Islands, 111-113, 115, 116
Berlin, 80
Bertrand, Alejandro, 105
Billinghurst, Guillermo, 64
Billinghurst-Latorre Protocol, 62
Blanco Encalada, 44, 48
Blanco Encalada, Manuel, 27
Blest Gana, Guillermo, 93
Boeta, Belisario, 55
Bolivia, 33, 34, 35, 36, 37, 38, 39, 40, 41,

126

Bolivia (continued), 42, 44, 45, 46, 48, 49, 51, 52, 53, 55, 56, 57, 58, 59, 62, 69, 95, 96, 106, 107
Bonapartists, 19
Bordeaux, 9
Boundary treaties, Chile and Argentina, arbitration agreement of 1877, 94-95, 96; Boundary Treaty of 1881, 95, 96-99, 101, 104, 105, 106, 107, 109, 110, 111; 1888 protocol, 102, 104, 105, 106; 1893 protocol, 104, 105, 106; 1896 agreement, 106; 1900 agreement, 111; 1902 agreements, 111, 116; 1938 arbitration agreement, 113
Boundary treaties, Chile and Bolivia, 1866, 36-37, 38, 42, 45; 1872 (Lindsay-Corral), 38; 1874, 38-39, 42, 43, 44, 45, 46
Brazil, 6, 7, 8, 9, 19, 41; Emperor of, 38
Brest, 77
Bristol, 78
Brunswick Peninsula, 90, 93
Buchanan, William J., 108
Buenos Aires, 14, 74, 75, 90, 91, 94, 96, 97, 99, 102, 103, 105, 107, 108, 109, 113; province, 91, 92, 96
Bulnes, Manuel, 34, 79, 80
cabildo abierto, 20, 21
Cabot, Sebastian, 4
Cáceres, Andrés, 53
Cádiz, 7; Cortes of, 19
Cajamarca, 53
Callao, 6, 7, 30, 31, 46, 47, 49, 51, 52, 54, 55, 79
Calvo, Pedro, 10
Calvo Encalada, Martin, 22
Camacho, Eleodoro, 48
Camarones River, 55

Cambiaso, José Miguel, 86, 87
Campero, Narciso, 48
Cañete, Marqués de, 6, 12
Canevaro, José Francisco, 45
Cape dos Bahias, 93
Cape Espíritu Santo, 94, 96, 111
Cape Forward, 82
Cape Horn, 26, 28, 29, 73, 90, 94, 98, 111
Cape San Domingo, 5
Cape Tamar, 82
Cape Virgins, 8, 97
Capital, la, province, 25
Caracoles, 37, 38
Carlota, Princess, 19
Carlotistas, 19
Carrera, Ignacio de la, 21
Carrera, José Miguel, 22, 23, 24
Carrera, Juan José, 22
Carrera, Luis, 22, 23
Castillo, Pedro del, 14
Castro, Chile, 84
casus foederis, 46
Cavendish, Thomas, 9
Ceballos, Pedro de, 14
cedulas (boundary), July 26, 1529, 3, 4; May, 1534, 4; Tucumán, 1563, 12; Strait, 1558, 13; Viceroyalty of Río de la Plata, 1776, 14
Centurion, Santos, 84
Chacaltana, Cesáreo, 63
Charcas, 14, 15; Audiencia of, 13
Charles I (of Spain), 3, 4, 9
Charles III (of Spain), 14, 15
Charles IV (of Spain), 18, 19
Charlottenburg, 80
Chilcayo, 65, 67
Chile, Audiencia of, 19, 20; junta, 21, 22; captain general, 31; captaincy general, 3, 18, 19, 20, 21, 109
Chile (Chilean navy), 78
Chile (Pacific Steam Navigation Com-

128

Joseph I (Bonaparte), 18, 19
Juana Pastora, 78
Juan Fernández Islands, 14, 26, 28, 29, 30, 31
Jufré, Juan, 14
Juries, 12
Justo de la Rivera, Jose, 84
Kellogg, Frank B., 70
King, Philip Parker, 73
King's Award, 110, 112, 114
Lacar, Lake, 110
Lackawana, 52
Ladrillero, Juan, 13
la Gasca, Pedro de, 12
Laguna del Desierto, 114, 115
Lanusse, Alejandro, 116
La Paz, 38, 43, 48, 55, 59, 70
Larrabure y Unanue, E., 61
Larrieu, Gabriel, 55
Las Damas Pass, 105
Lassiter Report, 69
Lassiter, William, 68
Lastorria, José Victoria, 92, 93
Lastra, Francisco de la, 23, 24
Lavalle, José Antonio, 45
League of Nations, 64
Lennox Island, 111, 112
Lima, 15, 35, 45, 48, 49, 51, 52, 54, 55, 61, 63, 70, 96, 115; Audiencia of, 12
Lindsay, Santiago, 38
Lircay, Battle of, 28, 84, 85; Treaty of, 24
Liverpool, 86
Loa River, 57,
Loaysa, Garcia Jofré, 3
Lobos Islands, 54
London, 9, 115
Londres, 13
Los Angeles, Battle of, 48
Los Patos Pass, 25

Louis Philippe, 77
Low, William, 78
Lozado, Cristobal, 83
Luque, Fernando, 4
Mabon, George, 77, 79, 81, 83
MacIver, Enrique, 108
Mackenna, Juan, 22, 23
Macnaghten, Lord Edward, 108
Madre de Dios, 5, 6
Magallanes, 84, 86, 87
Magdalena, city, 52; Island, 93
Magellan, Maritime Government, 85; territory, 31
Maissan, Louis, 82
Manco Capac, 46
Mapocho River, 11
Marco del Pont, Francisco Casimiro, 24
Mariana Islands, 77
Marin, Gaspar, 22
Marquesas Islands, 82
Martinez de Aldunate, José Antonio, 21
Martinez de Aldunate, Vicente, 19
Martinez de Rozas, Juan, 21, 22
Mary (of England), 13
Mas a Fuera Island, 31
Mas a Tierra Island, 31
Mejillones, 34, 36, 37, 39
Melgarejo, Mariano, 37, 43
Mendoza, city, 14, 24; province, 14, 91
Mendoza, Pedro de, 4, 5, 9, 10
Miller, Charles, 81
mineral deposits, 36, 37, 38, 43; copper, 33; silver, 33, 37; borax, 67; see nitrates
Miraflores, city, 49; Battle of, 49, 51
Mitre, Bartolomé, 92
Mocha, La, Island, 26, 28, 30
Molucca Islands (Spice Islands), 3, 4
Monteagudo, 79
Monte Marsan, 9

130

131

Última Esperanza, 110

Union, 47, 48

United States, 51, 53, 111; peace attempt, War of the Pacific, 51-52; arbitration of Tacna-Arica, 64-69; administration of Tacna-Arica plebiscit, 67-70; U.S. - Argentine Military Assistance Agreement, 114; Puna de Atacama arbitration, 107-108

Uriburu, José, 108

Urquiza, Justo José de, 91-92

Uruguay, 14, 55, 91

Ushuaia, Argentina, 116

Uspallata Pass, 25

uti posidetis of 1810, 34, 90, 92, 109, 110

Valderrama, Melquiades, 98, 99

Valdivia, city, 13, 23, 80; province, 27

Valdivia, Pedro de, 13, 27; early career, 11; expedition to Chile, 11; appointed governor of Chile, 11-12

Valencay, France, 18

Valera-Huneeus Protocol, 63, 64, 65

Valley of Aconcagua, 10

Valley of the Fountains, 8

Valparaiso, city, 12, 20, 30, 31, 55, 79, 83; province, 31

Velarde, Hernan, 64

Vendôme, Captain de, Vicomte de Béarne, 9

Venezuela, 11

Vera, Bernardo, 20

Vial Solar, Javier, 61

Victoria (of England), 76, 82, 108 110

Villagra, Francisco de, 12, 13, 14

Villanueva de la Serena, 11

Virasoro, Valentin, 103-105

Voladora, 84

War of the Pacific, 15, 38, 51, 69, 70, 73, 95, 96, 101, 102, 106; outbreak, 43-46; truce, Chile and Bolivia, 56-57; peace with Peru, 53-55; peace with Bolivia, 58-59

War with Spain, 35, 36, 39, 93

Washington, D. C., 51, 64, 69

Watering Place, 97

Wheelwright, William, 76

Williams, Horacio Luis, 79

Williams, John (Juan Guillermos), 78-79, 85; commands voyage to Strait, 79-83

Williams Rebolledo, Juan, 46

Windsor Castle, 9

World Court, 116

World War I, 64, 69, 112

World War II, 113